WRITING YEAR-END TEACHER

IMPROVEMENT PLANS

—RIGHT NOW!!

SECOND EDITION

WRITING YEAR-END TEACHER IMPROVEMENT PLANS

IMPROVEMENT PLANS

—RIGHT NOW!!

Cornelius L. Barker
Claudette J. Searchwell

SECOND EDITION

The
Principal's
Time-Saving
Reference
Guide

CORWIN PRESS
A SAGE Company

For information:

Corwin Press
A SAGE Company
2455 Teller Road
Thousand Oaks, California 91320
www.corwinpress.com

SAGE Ltd.
1 Oliver's Yard
55 City Road
London EC1Y 1SP
United Kingdom

SAGE India Pvt. Ltd.
B 1/I 1 Mohan Cooperative
    Industrial Area
Mathura Road, New Delhi 110 044
India

SAGE Asia-Pacific Pte. Ltd.
33 Pekin Street #02-01
Far East Square
Singapore 048763

Printed in the United States of America.

Library of Congress Cataloging-in-Publication Data

Barker, Cornelius L.
Writing year-end teacher improvement plans—right now!! : the principal's time-saving reference guide/Cornelius L. Barker, Claudette J. Searchwell. — 2nd ed.
     p. cm.
ISBN 978-1-4129-6372-5 (hardcover w/cd)
ISBN 978-1-4129-6373-2 (pbk. w/cd)
   1. Teachers—In-service training—United States—Handbooks, manuals, etc.
2. Teachers—Rating of—United States—Handbooks, manuals, etc. I. Searchwell, Claudette J. II. Title.

LB1731.B27 2009
371.14´4–dc22   2008030595

This book is printed on acid-free paper.

08   09   10   11   12   10   9   8   7   6   5   4   3   2   1

Acquisitions Editor:	Arnis Burvikovs
Associate Editor:	Desirée Enayati
Production Editor:	Eric Garner
Copy Editor:	Paula L. Fleming
Typesetter:	C&M Digitals (P) Ltd.
Proofreader:	Susan Schon
Cover Designer:	Michael Dubowe

CONTENTS

PREFACE TO THE SECOND EDITION

Planning, ongoing assessment, and evaluation are procedures inherent to the education profession. Each state, district, and school adopts methods designed to service its needs in carrying out these tasks. Very often, however, because of the lack of clear guidelines for interpreting success, progress was ill defined, and comparisons between districts and individual schools within them lacked symmetry.

The basic level of achievement considered standard for all students nationwide, as well as the quality of service given by the schools that they attend, has been established through the enactment of the No Child Left Behind Act of 2001. Through its mandate, all children must perform at or above grade level by the year 2014, and all instruction is to be delivered by highly qualified professionals.

The teaching effectiveness and the accountability for meeting mandates inherent in this law have resulted in states/districts formulating extensive strategies for compliance. Measurement of success takes various forms, requiring consideration of many variables. The year-end improvement plan, also known as the performance/personal improvement plan (PIP), is but one tool of the prerequisite assessment activity. It provides a view of present performance as well as a projection of future goals.

Writing Year-End Teacher Improvement Plans—Right Now!! is dedicated to the completion of this procedure in a qualitative, quantifiable, and purposeful manner. Administrative, supervisory, and teaching professionals will benefit from using this guide as an aide in chronicling present achievements and future goals.

The guide offers the following:

- 65 updated and revised proficiency categories
- New categories reflecting best practices
- An all-new comprehensive annual performance form package with diagnosis, report-of-progress, and summative assessment sections
- Forms containing comment sections for teachers and administrators to detail their partnership throughout the assessment process
- Added emphasis on how teachers and administrators can collaborate to evaluate and plan as a team

- A regrouped vocabulary resource organized by proficiency category
- New sample case studies

Writing Year-End Teacher Improvement Plans—Right Now!! will be extremely relevant and useful in completing the annual performance report, whatever the specific format/criteria used in your district.

ACKNOWLEDGMENTS

Corwin Press gratefully acknowledges the contributions of the following individuals:

Betsy Carter
Director of Mathematics, K–12
Hamden Public Schools
Hamden, CT

Brian E. Curtis
Assistant Principal
Cape Henlopen High School
Lewes, DE

Cary Dritz
Associate Superintendent
Ventura County Office of Education
Camarillo, CA

Michael Fisher
Critical Thinking Specialist
Starpoint Middle School
Lockport, NY

ABOUT THE AUTHORS

Cornelius L. Barker is a much sought-after lecturer for school and community groups on the subject of current cognitive and behavioral trends exhibited by today's youth. He served as a classroom teacher and as administrator in both elementary and secondary schools during his professional career.

In his retirement, he works with juveniles and young adults, using his extensive experience in research and lecturing with the at-risk population to reach, teach, and motivate his students to embrace education as a catalyst for restored hope and a positive perspective on life.

Claudette J. Searchwell recently concluded her second career as a member of the adjunct staff at Kean University in Union, New Jersey, serving as a clinical supervisor of preprofessional student teachers and precertification senior interns.

Her years of service in the field of education included positions as classroom teacher, assistant director of the federal Title I program, coordinator of citywide afterschool and summer programs, assistant principal, and principal.

INTRODUCTION

WHY IS THIS BOOK NEEDED?

Almost every situation that captures the attention, interest, and sensibilities of a society finds its way into the nation's schools.

Whether it be the opportunities and challenges of emerging technology or issues of health, social welfare, the economy, politics, and many more, schools have the responsibility of equipping students to meet the challenges of the 21st century successfully.

The No Child Left Behind Act of 2001 was enacted to promote and quantify accountability in obtaining this goal.

In fulfilling the objectives of this law, schools are charged with tangibly demonstrating that proficient people and excellent strategies are in place in accordance with specific guidelines . . . and that all children will be at grade level by 2014.

What training/experience does the educator bring to the table? How do current programs and procedures meet student needs? And, most important, to what degree of success do these factors come together for the benefit of the emotional, social, and academic growth of each and every student?

It is incumbent upon districts, schools, and individual education professionals to validate the efforts made toward addressing these issues by demonstrating compliance and successful achievement.

To this end, *Writing Year-End Teacher Improvement Plans—Right Now!!* is dedicated to the completion of comprehensive, professional teacher improvement plans. They can be thought of as "insurance policies," listing the teacher and education system as owners and the students as beneficiaries.

An improvement plan formula can be visualized as follows:

Successful Implementation of				
Stated Goals/Objectives	+	*Action Plan*	=	*Outcome(s)*
Student assessment data		Teaching strategies		Student achievement
National/district/ school initiatives		Persons responsible		Compliance with mandates
Professional objective(s)		Focused activities		Professional growth

This guide is an administrative tool—a template with which users, utilizing their district's format or the "Performance Progress and Improvement Plan" packet included in this book, as well as their ongoing observations, can construct the document that spells out the analysis of past performance and the plan for the coming year.

The essential components of assessing effective teaching and planning for ongoing professional growth includes recognizing and valuing observed strengths, determining areas where improvement is required, and suggesting specific actions to facilitate successful fulfillment of the stated goals and objectives.

Writing Year-End Teacher Improvement Plans—Right Now!! makes that process easy by providing a compact packet of forms, enabling the user to easily create a comprehensive, professional document that chronicles the teacher's annual journey toward the highest levels of proficiency.

Of course, the entire process can be completed in record time on each of the forms through the use of the upgraded interactive CD-ROM.

Just select, click, edit, save, and/or print . . . and the reports are ready!!

COMPONENTS AND INSTRUCTIONS

The "Performance Progress and Improvement Plan" is made up of five essential components:

1. Analysis of Teacher Performance (for the administrator)

2. Teacher Self-Assessment Form (for the teacher)

3. Recommendations for Improvement/Action Plan

4. Summative Report

5. Professional Development Report

1. Analysis of Teacher Performance

This form allows the administrator to point out those proficiency categories in which the teacher has shown consistent exemplary performance during the school year, as well as areas that need sustained improvement.

This can be done expeditiously by using the coded capabilities of the guide (e.g., if recorded under "Strengths," *14f* indicates that *the teacher has a thorough knowledge of curriculum content*).

In like manner, by recording *36c* in the "Areas Needing Improvement" section, the user states that *the teacher should regularly inform parents of student progress.*

2. Teacher Self-Assessment Form

The teacher is given the opportunity to record reflections on his or her performance during the year by using this form.

The teacher may create statements designating strengths and areas needing improvement. Or, using the glossary of terms (see Section 2) as a reference, the teacher may select areas of strength and those needing improvement by recording the corresponding category numbers and titles in the respective boxes.

The completed report is then presented to the administrator prior to the start of the annual performance plan process.

3. Recommendations for Improvement and Action Plan

Part Three allows the administrator to provide specific suggestions as to steps to take to strengthen the areas needing improvement.

4. Summative Report

In Part Four, teacher strengths are described, and the action plans that were suggested for areas needing improvement are evaluated as having been satisfactorily completed, needing ongoing improvement, or unsatisfactory.

5. Professional Development Report

Part Five allows the teacher to provide concrete proof of the steps taken toward attaining increased professional growth, as well as compliance with national and district mandates regarding proficiency.

PART I

The Essential Elements
of the Improvement Plan

This section contains

- 65 proficiency categories;
- a glossary of category terms; and
- 650 proficiency assessment statements with vocabulary aids.

SECTION 1

65 Proficiency Categories

This listing allows you to scan the proficiency categories quickly and choose the topics that best represent the competencies you wish to highlight and record.

1. Accountability
2. Administration
3. Affective Domain
4. Assessment
5. Behavior Modification
6. Brain-Based Learning
7. Clarity
8. Closure
9. Collaboration
10. Cooperative Learning
11. Creativity
12. Critical Thinking
13. Curriculum Delivery
14. Curriculum Knowledge (Knowledge of Content)
15. Curriculum Management
16. Discipline (Classroom Management)
17. Evaluation
18. Extracurricular Activities

19. Feedback to Students

20. Goal Setting for Students

21. Guidance

22. Instructional Delivery

23. Instructional Diversity

24. Leadership Skills

25. Learning Style (Multiple Intelligences)

26. Lesson Objectives

27. Managing Academic Diversity

28. Mandated Programs

29. Materials

30. Motivating Students

31. Motivating Students (Professional Practices)

32. Multiculturalism

33. Noninstructional Duties

34. Nontenured Teacher

35. Organization

36. Parents as Partners

37. Personal Attributes

38. Physical Plant (Creativity/Aesthetics)

39. Physical Plant (Instructional Space)

40. Planning (Lesson Plans)

41. Preparation for Delivery of Instruction

42. Preparation for Learning

43. Problem-Based Learning

44. Professional Development

45. Professional Habits (Personal)

46. Professional Habits (Workplace)

47. Rapport With Students

48. Record Keeping

49. Reflection

50. Relationship With Colleagues

51. Relationship With Parents and Community

52. School Climate (School Culture)

53. Self-Esteem (Students)

54. Self-Motivation (Students)

55. Special Needs (Special Education)

56. Standards and Practices

57. Student Behaviors

58. Students First

59. Supplemental Practices

60. Supporting Students

61. Teacher as Mentor

62. Technology (Professional Use)

63. Technology (Student Centered)

64. Test-Taking Skills

65. Time Management

SECTION 2

Glossary of Category Terms

This section provides an overview of the meaning and content of each proficiency category.

1. **Accountability:** Taking personal responsibility for professional performance

2. **Administration:** Sharing school mission and goals with administration

3. **Affective Domain:** Contributing to the emotional well-being of students

4. **Assessment:** Contributing to and measuring student achievement

5. **Behavior Modification:** Teaching strategies that promote positive student behaviors

6. **Brain-Based Learning:** Basing instruction on current research

7. **Clarity:** Using methods that make concepts clear to students

8. **Closure:** Concluding lessons and checking level of understanding

9. **Collaboration:** Working collegially to problem-solve

10. **Cooperative Learning:** Having students work within a group structure

11. **Creativity:** Using innovative teaching concepts and strategies

12. **Critical Thinking:** Promoting higher-order thinking in students

13. **Curriculum Delivery:** Teaching curriculum content effectively

14. **Curriculum Knowledge (Knowledge of Content):** Demonstrating mastery of subject matter

15. **Curriculum Management:** Using professional expertise to enhance curriculum content

16. **Discipline (Classroom Management):** Successfully managing student behavior

17. **Evaluation:** Taking a positive viewpoint regarding professional assessment

18. **Extracurricular Activities:** Participating in auxiliary school activities

19. **Feedback to Students:** Interacting with students regarding their work

20. **Goal Setting for Students:** Helping students look to the future

21. **Guidance:** Giving students individual attention

22. **Instructional Delivery:** Using effective teaching methods

23. **Instructional Diversity:** Enhancing instructional delivery

24. **Leadership Skills:** Demonstrating management capabilities

25. **Learning Styles (Multiple Intelligences):** Teaching students with varied strengths and talents

26. **Lesson Objectives:** Structuring goals and objectives

27. **Managing Academic Diversity:** Teaching students of varied abilities

28. **Mandated Programs:** Adhering to school, district, and national policies

29. **Materials:** Effective use of consumables/nonconsumables that support learning

30. **Motivating Students:** Using practices and demonstrating beliefs that inspire students to achieve

31. **Motivating Students (Professional Practices):** Stimulating students' academic achievement

32. **Multiculturalism:** Teaching in a global community

33. **Noninstructional Duties:** Performing services outside of instructional duties

34. **Nontenured Teacher:** Gaining experience and building confidence

35. **Organization:** Building a structured, organized professional environment

36. **Parents as Partners:** Enlisting teachers and parents as allies

37. **Personal Attributes:** Demonstrating a professional demeanor and actions

38. **Physical Plant (Creativity/Aesthetics):** Creating a vibrant, visually pleasing classroom environment

39. **Physical Plant (Instructional Space):** Maintaining a positive learning environment

40. **Planning:** Writing effective, comprehensive lesson plans

41. **Preparation for Delivery of Instruction (Teacher):** Using strategies that enhance teaching effectiveness

42. **Preparation for Learning (Students):** Using teacher-led anticipatory set activities

43. **Problem-Based Learning:** Leading students through problem-solving learning activities

44. **Professional Development:** Engaging in professional growth activities

45. **Professional Habits (Personal):** Demonstrating qualities and behaviors that enhance professional expertise.

46. **Professional Habits (Workplace):** Working both collegially and independently

47. **Rapport With Students:** Connecting with students on a humanistic level

48. **Record Keeping:** Managing professional data

49. **Reflection:** Assessing self-performance

50. **Relationship With Colleagues:** Acting as a valued member of the school community

51. **Relationship With Parents and Community:** Connecting to students' families and communities

52. **School Climate (School Culture):** Contributing to a sound classroom and school environment

53. **Self-Esteem (Students):** Helping students to feel good about themselves

54. **Self-Motivation (Students):** Empowering students

55. **Special Needs (Special Education):** Working effectively with students with disabilities

56. **Standards and Practices:** Following professional routines and practices

57. **Student Behaviors:** Using teacher strategies resulting in sound student behaviors

58. **Students First:** Valuing and uplifting students

59. **Supplemental Practices:** Supporting varied student activities

60. **Supporting Students:** Facilitating the learning experience for students

61. **Teacher as Mentor:** Sharing expertise, time, and effort for the good of the school

62. **Technology (Professional Use):** Using technology as an effective teaching tool

63. **Technology (Student-Centered):** Managing student use of technology as a learning tool

64. **Test-Taking Skills:** Enhancing students' test-taking skills

65. **Time Management:** Maximizing time for instructional delivery

SECTION 3

650 Proficiency Assessment Statements With Vocabulary Aids

This section presents the core of *Writing Year-End Teacher Improvement Plans—Right Now!!* Following are the 65 proficiency categories from Section 1 and ten accompanying assessment statements for each of the categories (for a total of 650), along with a useful vocabulary list for each segment to help you edit your statements.

1. ACCOUNTABILITY

a. Accept (responsibility, accountability) for improved student learning.

b. Students exceed basic performance objectives as a result of your teaching.

c. Exhibit a willingness to accept responsibility for student outcomes.

d. Identify constraints that hinder student progress and take steps to remedy those constraints.

e. Practice self-reflection and encourage students to do the same.

f. Assess effectiveness of instruction via (follow-up activities, quizzes, tests, feedback from students, formative assessments).

g. Explore current theories and practices regarding (professional accountability, performance-based compensation).

h. Demonstrate a willingness to participate in professional initiatives and take responsibility for reaching sound outcomes.

i. Follow teaching activities through to a logical conclusion and evaluate outcomes.

j. Participate fully within the larger school community and share (accountability, responsibility) for school-based initiatives.

Vocabulary List

absorb	examine	results
answerability	follow through	search
carry out	go beyond	shares
collaborate	idea	show
compliance	meet	solution
conclusion	remediate	take part in
culpable	resolution	test
evaluate	resolve	think

2. ADMINISTRATION

a. Engage in ongoing, meaningful dialogue with administrators regarding student achievement.

b. Develop a shared sense of purpose through collaborative interaction with (administrators, supervisors).

c. (Implement, Apply) administrative (suggestions, initiatives) in a timely and effective manner.

d. Remain open to administrative suggestions for professional improvement and perform duties in a manner consistent with administrative requests.

e. Work effectively with administrators to reach school objectives.

f. Develop a positive rapport with the administrative staff.

g. Take advantage of opportunities to collaborate with administrators regarding (curriculum, materials, equipment, resources, physical plant, student discipline, school mission, school objectives, school climate, special events).

h. Act in accordance with administrative and/or district (guidelines, policies, suggestions, requests).

i. Respect and support the principal's role in the school organization.

j. Implement constructive suggestions provided by administrators and/ or supervisory personnel during/after (conferences, observations, evaluations).

Vocabulary List

aid	concern	join with
alliance with	concur	loyal to
authority	connection	meet with
belief	course of action	realize
benefit from	familiarity	responsive to
communicate	group	support
compliance	help	team player
comply with	join forces	understanding

3. AFFECTIVE DOMAIN

a. Treat students with dignity and respect.

b. Maintain a value-oriented classroom in which students feel prized and nurtured.

c. Build character in your lessons through incorporation of tenets of (self-discipline, cultural appreciation, valuing self and others).

d. Anticipate student needs and render appropriate assistance when necessary.

e. Maintain a positive rapport with students.

f. Communicate effectively with students, using language they can understand.

g. Create a network of assistance for students through (peer liaisons, mentors, counselors).

h. (Maintain, Have) an interest in the development of each student and treat each student as a unique and valued individual.

i. Provide help, support, and encouragement to all students.

j. Facilitate the rapid assimilation of new students into the (classroom, school).

Vocabulary List

acknowledge	connect with	integrity
aid	develop	make available
attitude	ease	meet with
backing	empathize with	respect
bolster	feeling tone	show consideration
caring	foresee	support
collegial	grace	supportive
concern	help	value

4. ASSESSMENT

a. Utilize (formative, summative) assessment data to (differentiate, plan) (individualized, group) (support, delivery of instruction).

b. Use authentic assessment (tools, strategies) with corresponding rubrics to assess (competency, growth, mastery).

c. Help students to (reflect on, strategize) their (performance, work, outcomes).

d. Modify future lesson plans based on analysis of formative assessment data.

e. Become (knowledgeable of, well versed in) the content of (state, district) mandated standardized tests.

f. Formulate tests that reflect (content, objectives) that were taught.

g. Use a variety of evaluation strategies, including (student self-assessments, oral recitation, visual presentations, narratives, research projects, technological presentations, peer review, portfolio assessment, group assessment, collegial review).

h. Develop appropriate rubrics to assess comprehension and mastery accurately.

i. Upgrade evaluation criteria to sustain a high level of student motivation and achievement.

j. Collaborate with specialists to assess student (needs, progress, aptitudes, strengths, weaknesses).

Vocabulary List

abilities	judge	record
account for	log	review
benchmarks	make use of	rules
capabilities	meet with	standards
evaluate	promote	statistics
goals	prompt	teacher-made
incorporate	range	test
information	real-life	value

5. BEHAVIOR MODIFICATION

a. Develop cooperatively with student a clearly stated behavioral contract that includes stated goals and objectives, a system of consequences for noncompliance, a time line for achieving goals, monitoring guidelines, and provisions for making refinements or revisions.

b. (Encourage, Allow, Insist on) students (to reflect, reflecting) on and (learn, learning) from their mistakes.

c. Hold students accountable for their (actions, decisions, choices).

d. Devise and implement effective behavior modification techniques, including (positive reinforcement, assertive discipline, moral/character education, conflict resolution, anger management, peer mediation, socialization techniques, system of rewards and consequences, behavioral contracts).

e. Anticipate factors that negatively impact student (behavior, academic achievement, development) and act proactively to avoid their negative influence.

f. Identify social conflict between students and listen to and adjudicate grievances promptly.

g. Enforce behavior modification to protect students' dignity and self-esteem and maintain a positive classroom culture.

h. Develop and implement classroom activities that engage students and deflect the possibility of their (participating, engaging) in acting-out behaviors.

i. Clearly define and articulate (classroom, school, district) standards of behavior to students and their parents.

j. Devise and implement system of recognition rewards for students who demonstrate positive behaviors including (commendations sent home, participation in award assemblies, in-class honors and awards).

Vocabulary List

agreement	errors	repentant
authority	explain	respect for others
be aware of	guideline	responsible for
climate	instill	self-confidence
communicate	judge	set up
conduct	limitations	supervise
control	outcomes	sway
cooperate with	prevent	together with

6. BRAIN-BASED LEARNING

a. (Plan, Prepare, Deliver) an array of (assignments, lessons) representative of fundamental principles of how the brain works, including, but not limited to, providing a relaxed and nurturing physical environment, varied resources, flexible learning, immersion in curriculum content via (unit, authentic) learning experiences, allowing time to process information, incorporation of the arts, etc.

b. Allow students to (experience, work through) an array of diverse activities.

c. Assess (understanding, growth, mastery) based on rubrics specific to differentiated tasks.

d. Establish (ability groups, tiers, flexible grouping) to (manage, accommodate) students in a mixed-ability setting.

e. Create a thematic-based curriculum, offering a range of educational (experiences, challenges).

f. Utilize authentic assessment strategies as (tools, indicators) of (progress, mastery) that accommodate students' learning styles.

g. Administer (periodic, frequent) mini-assessments to gauge (comprehension, growth, appropriateness) of the program for learning.

h. (Deliver, Create) lessons that allow students to participate in (authentic, meaningful, experiential) learning activities.

i. Maintain a classroom environment where students' capabilities are nurtured and disabilities are (accepted, minimized).

j. Provide a rich, artistic, and multisensory learning environment that encourages (risk taking, experimentation, problem solving).

Vocabulary List

accommodate	generate	situations
adapt	integrate	specialized
arrange	levels	standards
assorted	materials	subject matter
assortment	permit	talents
cooperative groups	real-life	teacher-made
determine	selection	test
devise	set up	valid

7. CLARITY

a. Divide learning into (doable, manageable) segments.

b. Integrate authentic, student-identified (themes, scenarios) into assignments.

c. Heighten clarity of lesson content through the use of (anecdotes, analogies, diagrams, review of prior learning, modeling of expected behavior/outcomes, visual/auditory aids, role-playing, technology, etc.).

d. Clarify and reinforce skills to be taught.

e. Present information in a logical and concise (manner, sequence).

f. Be considerate of and responsive to student questions.

g. Provide information that is (current, accurate, appropriate) for student ability levels.

h. Set forth clear, focused (benchmarks, criteria) for student (achievement, success, progress).

i. Clearly define core concepts of the subject matter.

j. Give clear directions and explanations.

Vocabulary List

agree to	emphasize	model
aid	enable	plainly
articulate	explain	real-life
basic	facilitate	review
comprehensible	give	simplify
convey	in order	supplementary material
core	introduce	systematic
devise	make available	understandable

8. CLOSURE

a. (Critique, Review) the salient points of information presented during the lesson.

b. Dispense homework related to current classroom topics and targeted to student (needs, deficiencies, strengths).

c. Manage time to allow for (closure, summary) activities and assign follow-up work based on student needs after (the lesson, summative assessment).

d. Conduct (closure, summary) activities throughout the lesson as new information is introduced.

e. Develop a variety of ways to (summarize, assess the understanding of, reinforce major points of) newly acquired information and skills.

f. Review key elements of the lesson and conduct relevant closure activities.

g. Conduct closure activities that support the lesson objectives.

h. Check frequently for understanding during the course of the lesson.

i. Evaluate the effectiveness of the lesson based on the extent to which goals were achieved.

j. Allow sufficient time for students to practice newly acquired skills and to demonstrate mastery.

Vocabulary List

acknowledges	facilitate	perspective
adjust	guide	positive attitude
articulate	incorporate	problem solving
constructive	involvement	respect
cooperates	mechanics	tact
demonstrate	open-mindedness	understanding
encourage	opportunity	vision
engage	patience	visualize

9. COLLABORATION (PROFESSIONAL LEARNING COMMUNITY)

a. Be candid, cogent, and concise when communicating your (point of view, position, ideas).

b. Maintain a (demeanor, tone) of compromise when interacting (with others, within the collegial group).

c. (Clarify, Fully comprehend) (expectations, objectives, goals, positions, mandates) of the task before forming conclusion(s).

d. (Develop, Become comfortable with) the personal components of collaboration, including (cooperation, trust, commitment, competence, collegiality).

e. Convey (an interest in, competence in, knowledge of) the (subject, mission, assignment, task) during (collaboration, cohort) (meetings, sessions).

f. Respect the time, effort, and input of others on the team.

g. Enhance student learning through shared (planning, research, project work) with colleagues.

h. Remain open to (negotiation, compromise) as a viable problem-solving strategy.

i. Remain comfortable in our school culture where collaboration is key.

j. Remain highly engaged and productive during team (sessions, meetings).

Vocabulary List

character	enthusiastic	peer review
constructive	incorporate	periodicals
current issues	journal	provide
decision-making	knowledgeable	research
demonstrate	mechanics	resolution
direct	motivate	self-analytical
display	opportunity	self-reflective
encourage	participate	vitality

10. COOPERATIVE LEARNING

a. Establish cooperative learning groups based on your knowledge of students' (learning styles, abilities, skill levels, interests).

b. Set (goals, rules, standards) for (individual, group) (productivity, interaction).

c. Conduct interim assessments based on observed (individual, group) (achievement, progress, input) as the group work progresses.

d. (Build, Support, Strengthen) positive qualities of interdependence in the students, including (encouragement, assistance, support, sharing, etc.).

e. Utilize (rubrics, weighted ratings) to attach value to individual contributions to the group effort.

f. (Manage, Monitor) interpersonal behaviors between students to (promote, sustain) positive group (interaction, productivity).

g. Give students insight into "how the world works" through their cooperative learning experiences.

h. Increase student performance in (comprehension, problem solving) through their work in cooperative learning groups.

i. Give students clear directions as to the (task, assignment, individual roles, expected outcomes) at the onset of the cooperative group activity.

j. (Assess, Recognize, Reward) (individual, team) (performance, productivity) through the awarding of (grades, points, certificates, praise, awards, etc.).

Vocabulary List

articulate	explore	recognition
assistance	growth	respond
attention	insight	self-worth
build	motivation	solution
clarify	participate	strengths
constructive	performance	study habits
demeanor	potential	tests
effect	promotes	time management

11. CREATIVITY

a. Realize the value of effectively incorporating the arts into classroom projects.

b. Plan and initiate activities that rival and surpass the (lure, thrill, excitement) of (TV, video games).

c. Provide (time, opportunities, inspiration, freedom) that enable(s) students to express their creativity.

d. Attend (workshops, classes, demonstrations) that provide (innovative, creative) (ideas, approaches) to lesson activities.

e. Investigate creative (projects, ideas, activities) by making use of professional (magazines, journals, publications, Web sites).

f. Make subject matter "come alive" through the use of (innovative, creative) (projects, materials, approaches).

g. Consult with (colleagues, specialists) to gain (insight, ideas, assistance) for planning creative lesson activities.

h. Build on innovative (programs, lessons, activities, techniques, strategies) to promote student interest in (learning, the subject matter).

i. Plan and implement a (project-based, problem-based, thematic unit) approach to instruction.

j. Use vivid and expressive language to enhance the learning experience for students.

Vocabulary List

arrange	demonstrate	opportunity
attitude	develop	order
cleanliness	displays	organization
compromise	environment	plan
computers	influence	prepare
concern	inspirational	productive
contribute	learning styles	respect
control	manner	technology

12. CRITICAL THINKING

a. Challenge students to (discover, work through) component elements of a task after being given the "big picture."

b. Require students to (reflect upon, support) their (response, conclusion, viewpoint).

c. (Model, Generate, Engage students in) (projects, activities) requiring them to (solve, explore) solutions to real-life problems.

d. Help students develop critical-thinking skills, including forming questions, making judgments, identifying assumptions.

e. Pose questions requiring (open-ended, higher-order) thinking.

f. Expose students to (problem solving, thinking and reasoning, decision making, inquiry) by infusing these skills into lessons.

g. Require students to share their reasoning processes by elaborating on their answers.

h. Pose thought-provoking (follow-up, exploratory, motivational) questions.

i. Organize lessons so that critical thinking is a natural extension of lesson activities.

j. Help students develop analytical problem-solving skills and work through complex concepts to reach logical conclusions.

Vocabulary List

analyzing	enhance	promote
appropriate	enrichment	resource
closure	evaluation	review
cognitive development	focus	self-directed
comprehension	follow-up	summative
cooperative learning	group activities	supplementary
development	learning styles	support
elicit	problem solving	utilize

13. CURRICULUM DELIVERY

a. (Review, Assess) teaching effectiveness and make adjustment(s) where needed.

b. Provide opportunities for students to use information-gathering skills to problem solve.

c. Display (enthusiasm, resourcefulness) when delivering instruction.

d. Ensure that students actively participate during the delivery of instruction.

e. Use (hands-on instruction, whole-class instruction, cooperative learning, technology, learning centers, thematic units, group/individualized/research projects) to enhance instruction.

f. Teach for cognitive (understanding, mastery).

g. Deliver lessons in a logical sequence.

h. (Begin lesson, Teach) at a concrete level of comprehension, using (manipulatives, diagrams, maps, audiovisual devices, computers, demonstrations, experiments, literature).

i. Instruct at an abstract level of comprehension, allowing students to discover outcomes.

j. Facilitate successful learning outcomes by providing (hands-on instruction, creative approaches to learning, assignments geared toward learning styles).

Vocabulary List

activities	implement	relevant
A/V equipment	maximize	research
classroom materials	photographs	re-teach
complete	plan	review
computers	posters	submit
display	projects	technology
engage	reinforcement	workbooks
homework	related charts	worksheets

14. CURRICULUM KNOWLEDGE (KNOWLEDGE OF CONTENT)

a. (Gain knowledge of, Develop acumen with) (skills, curriculum, instructional areas) outside your regular (teaching assignment, area[s] of responsibility).

b. Select standards for achievement based on the required curriculum, prior knowledge, and student needs.

c. Review and absorb the entire year's curriculum goals at the beginning of the term.

d. Utilize grade-level (curriculum, core curriculum) guides as the basis for planning.

e. (Incorporate, Master) adaptations to the curriculum as required.

f. (Gain, Develop) a thorough knowledge of the curriculum content.

g. Supplement professional material used as the basis for (planning, teaching) to ensure that the curriculum content is current, relevant, and sufficient to provide students with a rich learning experience.

h. Develop and maintain an awareness of new developments in curriculum content of (pilot programs, computer software) to expose students to information beyond the textbook.

i. Use (metaphors, symbols, examples, experiments, discussion, audiovisuals) to shed light on curriculum content and to ensure student understanding.

j. Make certain that the curriculum (offers, reflects, contains) perspectives that reflect the (multicultural, global) society in which your students live.

Vocabulary List

align	effective	proficient in
analysis	evaluation	required
analyze	interpretation	sequential
application	knowledge	standards
approved	mandate	synthesis
available	practiced in	textbook
cogent manner	prescribe	translation
delineate	proficiencies	unit

15. CURRICULUM MANAGEMENT

a. Infuse character building education into the (lesson, curriculum).

b. Apply the scientific process of observation, experimentation, investigation, recording, and analysis into varied subjects.

c. Carry out a seamless flow between lesson (components, activities).

d. Develop and display a strong knowledge of (curriculum content, pedagogy).

e. Utilize technology-based instruction.

f. Follow the approved district (curriculum guides, teacher manuals, program guides) when planning instruction.

g. Demonstrate the ability to master new (texts, techniques, technologies, materials, curricula, programs, concepts) quickly.

h. Become current with new instructional (methods, materials, programs).

i. Explain and model essential lesson concepts, expected skills, and outcomes to students.

j. Become conversant with state, district, and school curriculum guidelines.

Vocabulary List

communicate	district goals	realistic approach
content	expectation	requirements
core standards	knowledge of	school goals
correlation	learning task	scope
definition	mandates	sequence
demonstrate	model	subject matter
description	overview	synopsis
direction	readiness	transfer

16. DISCIPLINE (CLASSROOM MANAGEMENT)

a. Exude quiet strength and provide a structured environment in which your students can thrive.

b. Gain training to (recognize signs, provide intervention) for (at-risk, troubled) students.

c. (Confer, Cooperate) with others to (remedy, cope with, understand) the needs of (troubled, at-risk) students.

d. Help students develop coping skills to manage their (day-to-day, life) experiences better.

e. Teach students to support their (beliefs, opinions) in non-(combative, argumentative, retaliatory) ways.

f. Skillfully intervene and (defuse, resolve) crisis situations.

g. Maintain a positive classroom environment and contribute to an orderly school culture by upholding clearly stated rules, demonstrating mutual respect with students, and keeping them actively engaged in positive and productive classroom activities.

h. Quell off-task behaviors (unobtrusively, effectively, rapidly) and in a manner that maintains the dignity and feelings of students and the calmness of the classroom environment.

i. (Collaborate with colleagues, Research using the Internet, Attend workshops, Read professional literature, etc.) to build a repertoire of effective classroom management techniques.

j. Consistently enforce (district, school, classroom) rules and regulations.

Vocabulary List

behavior modification	deflect	maintain
behaviors	dialogue	mediation
conducive	eliminate	order
control	environment	recognize
cooperative grouping	handle	response
coping with	implement	responsibility
correct	inappropriate	rules
decorum	intervention	transition

17. EVALUATION

a. Welcome (observation, analysis, critiques) of your teaching performance.

b. Maintain a comprehensive professional portfolio that includes (academic, scholarly) (research, pursuits) and teaching (progress, development).

c. Work to satisfy all (licensing, incentive, tenure) mandates.

d. Objectively consider (merit pay, performance-based compensation) as it pertains to professional accountability.

e. Practice self-reflection to assess the quality of your professional performance.

f. Remain open to constructive criticism and act upon needed change.

g. Prepare for and cooperate with (peer reviews, informal/formal evaluations, constructive suggestions).

h. Strive to attain professional excellence status within (state, local, administrative) guidelines.

i. Self-assess the value of your teaching performance based upon (classroom effectiveness, student achievement).

j. (Internalize, Acknowledge) the range of professional competencies that are (contained in the, considered during the) evaluation process.

Vocabulary List

academic growth	growth	record
adjust	lesson components	select
administer	mastery	self-assessment
assess	measure	skills array
comprehension	monitor	subject matter
determine	overt responses	test
effectiveness	practice test	test-taking skills
employ	progress	understanding

18. EXTRACURRICULAR ACTIVITIES

a. Willingly participate in (afterschool, community, schoolwide) activities and take an opportunity to (extend, cement) relationships with (colleagues, students, parents) outside of the classroom.

b. Benefit from involvement in professional extracurricular activities, such as interacting with others of like mind/interests; furthering professional expertise; building resume data; showing commitment; sharing abilities and time with others with same interests; learning leadership, management, and support skills; utilizing opportunities to help others; etc.

c. (Volunteer, Agree) to perform additional duties upon request.

d. Participate in extracurricular activities in a voluntary and dedicated spirit of helpfulness and school spirit.

e. Closely monitor student activities to ensure student (success, safety).

f. Volunteer to participate in (school, district, community) activities off the school campus to cement alliances with students, parents, and the community.

g. Join and participate in the school parent/teacher organization.

h. Act as a mentor, chaperone, and cheerleader as students engage in (activities, contests, competitions, events).

i. Willingly fill the role as a (tutor, mentor, advisor, confidante, coach).

j. Assist (teacher interns, new teachers, volunteers, paraeducators) with all phases of their (interaction, work) with students.

Vocabulary List

accommodate	experiments	productive
aid	facilitate	recognition
apprenticeship	flexibility	school-based
athletics	imagination	special project
contribute	innovation	training program
creativity	integrity	unrelenting
debate	organizations	unselfish
experiential	plan	volunteer

19. FEEDBACK TO STUDENTS

a. Share test results with students in (language, a manner) they (can understand, find helpful).

b. Check for understanding and (reinforce, review, reteach) lessons when necessary.

c. Provide timely feedback on (assignments, tests, quizzes, homework, class work, projects, written work, performance, grades).

d. Offer students constructive suggestions regarding their work.

e. Provide students with a frank analysis of their (work, skills, accomplishments, strengths, weaknesses).

f. Reward (good grades, effort, growth) with praise to strengthen positive outcomes.

g. Honor student responses and offer commendations for the (quality, effort shown) (of, in) their participation.

h. Utilize e-mail to (review, discuss) class work with students.

i. Regularly check student (assignments, research projects, notebooks, journals, portfolios) and provide written and/or oral feedback.

j. Monitor ongoing student progress (during classes, during independent work, during participation in cooperative groups, while working at learning centers).

Vocabulary List

ability	efforts	refrain
acceptance	improvement	study habits
achievement	isolation	support
applaud	maintain	test-taking
attain	opinionated	time management
collaboration	participate	understand
contribution	question	validate
critical thinking	recognize	value

20. GOAL SETTING FOR STUDENTS

a. Identify and nurture students' talents beyond grades and test scores.

b. (Encourage, Help) students meet and exceed (national, district, school) (requirements, mandates).

c. Challenge and guide students to achieve (high, realistic, challenging) goals.

d. Encourage students to take responsibility for their own improvement.

e. Inspire students to (learn, achieve, excel, explore, persevere, set goals).

f. Help students develop (short-, long-) term (academic, personal, career) goals.

g. Devise and enter into (learning, behavioral, achievement, performance) contracts with students.

h. Emphasize the importance of excellent (attendance, punctuality, academic achievement, conduct) and its relationship to achievement and success.

i. Encourage student achievement by implementing incentive programs.

j. Help students identify and connect with (acceptable, available) role models.

Vocabulary List

accomplishment	instruction	potential
actualize	interest in	produce
comprehend	mastery	promote
demonstrate	motivate	reach
expectation	opportunity	recognition
independence	outcomes	reflect
innovative	participate	self-evaluation
inspire	performance-base	variety

21. GUIDANCE

a. Help students develop (behaviors, skills) equipping them to participate and succeed in/on the (culture of work, world community, next academic level).

b. Make appropriate referrals for students to receive services and follow-up support.

c. Serve as (mentor, counselor, friend, advisor) to students.

d. Stress the benefits of students applying their (innate, intuitive) talents.

e. Examine the individual needs and interests of students and challenge them to achieve their goals.

f. Increase your awareness concerning the many responsibilities involved in working with students and the positive impact your active involvement can make.

g. Stress (sound health practices, safety, responsible behavior, a positive outlook, fitness) to your students.

h. Teach students to work (independently, in groups) in an organized and focused manner.

i. Encourage students to become caring, responsible, constructive, and motivated contributors.

j. Help students search for and obtain sources of (financial aid, academic tutoring, mentoring, support).

Vocabulary List

adopt	incorporate	pacing
build	inspects	patience
check	interact	planning
constructive	involve	reinforce
correct	mechanics	routine
develop	monitor	supplemental
encourage	motivate	supportive
high expectation	motivational	teach

22. INSTRUCTIONAL DELIVERY

a. Speak to students—not at them.

b. Use a variety of teaching methods including (cooperative learning, computer-assisted learning, problem-based instruction, etc.).

c. Gain greater proficiency in conveying lesson content.

d. Use (lecture, chalkboard illustrations, question-and-answer sessions, whole/small-group discussion, thematic units, learning centers, audiovisual presentations, computer-assisted learning, cooperative grouping) as a teaching (method, strategy).

e. Provide individualized instruction and actively involve students in the learning process.

f. Show the interrelatedness of subject matter by using thematic units as a teaching strategy.

g. Modify teaching (method, strategies, plans) when necessary.

h. Check for comprehension during the lesson and adjust teaching when necessary.

i. Involve students in problem-based learning as a (process, exercise) to stimulate independent thinking.

j. Use instructional strategies that have positive impacts on student learning.

Vocabulary List

activities	effective	measurable
alternative	ethical	process
assess	expectation	progress
attainable	feeling tone	projects
concern	flexible	remains
consistent	hands-on	re-teach
creative	learning styles	revised
discussion	manipulative	sequence

23. INSTRUCTIONAL DIVERSITY

a. (Plans, Activities, Teaching strategies) evolve as change is warranted.

b. (Offer, Prepare) an assortment of assignments based on graduated levels of (difficulty, complexity, skill ability, challenge).

c. Match assignments to (learning styles, abilities) of individual students.

d. Enhance (textbook, workbook, chapter) information through the use of supplementary material.

e. Avoid reliance on (textbook, worksheets) as the sole source of instruction.

f. Provide a variety of learning experiences, allowing students to think beyond the limits of the textbook.

g. Stimulate student participation by incorporating hands-on activities into the lesson.

h. Pace instruction so student involvement is neither rushed nor delayed.

i. Remain mindful of individual student (talents, needs, learning styles, personalities, abilities) when forming groups.

j. Dare to be innovative.

Vocabulary List

adjust	encourage	outcomes
clarify	expectations	participate
communicate	flexible	problem solve
conducive	focus	provides
contribute	implement	respond
cooperative	measure	share
critical thinking	monitor	stimulate
effective	optimum	well-maintained

24. LEADERSHIP SKILLS

a. Consider assuming a role of (leader, facilitator) in collaborative groups.

b. (Present, Articulate) problems with possible solutions in mind.

c. (Increase your, Gain) empowerment by increasing your decision-making abilities.

d. Be willing to (solve problems, meet challenges) independently as well as collectively.

e. Show a willingness to assume a leadership role in school (projects, activities, organization, grade-level meetings).

f. Develop your leadership skills to play a greater role in school program initiatives and to make a greater impact in performing as a change agent.

g. Show willingness to assume greater responsibility for improving the school climate.

h. Apply for grants designed to further professional goals and enhance the school program.

i. Participate fully in (professional, school, peer review, site-based management) activities.

j. Demonstrate an ability and a willingness to effect positive change.

Vocabulary List

adept	exhibit	responsible
assist	input	self-analytical
collegially	maintain	self-reflective
consults	participates	shares
decision maker	persevere	strives
empathy	professionalism	support
encourages	proficient	vitality
enthusiastic	rapport	volunteer

25. LEARNING STYLES (MULTIPLE INTELLIGENCES)

a. Adapt instruction to support the way students learn and what they need.

b. Engage students through offering a range of learning experiences from which to choose.

c. (Develop, Accommodate) students' intelligences through (refining, individualizing) material(s) and adjusting teaching methods.

d. Implement strategies to accommodate learning styles through (team-teaching, unit study, project-based activities, supplemental materials, etc.).

e. Research proven authorities on the subject of multiple intelligences.

f. Acknowledge the various learning styles of students when (posing questions, planning, assessing progress).

g. Recognize and meet the needs of students of varied intelligences, including (verbal, kinesthetic, musical, naturalist, logical-mathematical, interpersonal, intrapersonal, visual).

h. Maintain a differentiated classroom that offers various routes to learning.

i. Gain knowledge of the (academic, social, emotional) development and principles of learning related to (preschool, primary, elementary, middle, secondary, special needs) students.

j. Devise plans that reflect knowledge of the (varied learning styles, multiple intelligences, basic skills, special needs) of students.

Vocabulary List

accurately	enthusiasm for	respond
articulate	evaluation	solution
assistance	explore	strengths
clarify	insight	study habits
comment	positive	support
concerns	question	time management
constructive	readily	weaknesses
counseling	remediation	willingly

26. LESSON OBJECTIVES (LEARNING OBJECTIVES)

a. (Review, Construct) the lesson objective to ensure that learning outcomes that reflect (what students need, how students learn, core curriculum standards, movement toward broader goals/outcomes) have been included.

b. Write clearly defined, comprehensive, and neat lesson plans that contain (skills, activities, materials, time lines, expected outcomes).

c. Teach to the objectives of the lesson.

d. Explain the purpose, scope, and expected goals of the lesson to the students.

e. Develop effective short- and long-term objectives.

f. Use the students' frame of reference when planning to facilitate greater understanding of lesson content.

g. Align all activities with the lesson objectives.

h. Formulate objectives that confirm the ability to plan for varied abilities, intelligences, and learning styles within the (traditional, inclusive) classroom.

i. Structure written lesson objectives in which the three main components are congruent, including the objective/task, a standard evaluation, and criteria for acceptable performance.

j. Write objectives on all levels of the cognitive behavior steps of Bloom's taxonomy, including knowledge, comprehension, application, analysis, synthesis, and evaluation.

Vocabulary List

analysis	delivery	learning styles
application	evaluation	problem-solving
assist	focus	question
cogent manner	hands-on materials	research
cognitive development	homework	sequential
comprehension	intellectual abilities	synthesis
critical thinking	interpretation	teacher-integrated
cross-content	knowledge	translation

27. MANAGING ACADEMIC DIVERSITY

a. Become knowledgeable about child development learning stages.

b. Give students of varied ability opportunities to contribute to team success through cooperative learning involvement.

c. Assess (contributions, growth, performance) of individual students (to, in) cooperative learning groups.

d. Remain sensitive to students' academic needs to address individual differences in the mixed-ability classroom.

e. Regroup students when necessary.

f. Plan lessons in which various student learning styles are considered.

g. Create and apply (differentiated curriculum, flexible time use, alternative assessment strategies, varied assignments, varied grading patterns) that support the individual abilities/patterns of learning of students.

h. Conduct frequent assessments of student progress and initiate instructional intervention where needed.

i. Provide tiered assignments that begin at comfortable ability levels and gradually increase in difficulty as new skills are (introduced, mastered).

j. Motivate students by making learning tasks/assignments relevant to their interests.

Vocabulary List

academic achievement	encourage	participate
assistance	experience	progress
background	feedback	provide
communicate	higher achievement	recognize
contribution	information	relate
cooperation	interest	support
creative	life experiences	talent
differences	needs	validate

28. MANDATED PROGRAMS

a. (Build, Maintain) a professional portfolio outlining conformance with the No Child Left Behind Act (NCLB) proficiency requirements.

b. Continually (evolve, grow) professionally to meet increasing (technological, NCLB, best practice) (mandates, requirements).

c. Keep abreast of and comply with local, state, and federal guidelines for teaching performance.

d. Adequately prepare students for standardized tests.

e. Maintain a professional portfolio that reflects professional skills and accomplishments.

f. Comply with district and state professional development mandates.

g. Participate fully in (schoolwide, districtwide, out-of-district) professional development activities.

h. Address national, state, and local curriculum standards when planning and delivering instruction.

i. Collaborate with specialists responsible for providing services to your students.

j. Take an active role in comprehensive (school reform, management by objective) initiatives.

Vocabulary List

approved	expert in	regulations
consistent	follow	required
content	interschool activities	resource
core curriculum	knowledgeable of	routine
course of study	policy	school mission
devise	practiced in	standards
district mission	prescribed	teaching methods
enforce	proficient in	Whole-School Reform

29. MATERIALS

a. (Maintain, Organize, Stock) classroom learning centers with materials that are highly (relevant, compatible) with independent, goal-driven activities.

b. Provide resources geared to (enhance, support) (learning opportunities, lesson objectives, instructional goals, student learning styles).

c. Provide a variety of appropriate supplemental materials to support the (curriculum, topic, subject, unit, theme) currently being taught.

d. Provide supplementary material appropriate to student developmental levels, including adapting materials for inclusion of students.

e. Take an active role in (piloting, ordering, assessing) new curriculum materials.

f. Incorporate audiovisual material and technology into the lesson.

g. Update resource materials and use them in a timely manner to enhance curriculum content.

h. Give students responsibility for the efficient handling and maintenance of (classroom, personal) materials.

i. Utilize hands-on instructional materials that engage students cognitively and physically.

j. Formulate lists of Web sites offering a wide range of usable informational tools giving access to current teaching/learning (strategies, aids, concepts, etc.).

Vocabulary List

A/V equipment	library	software
books/texts	maintenance	student work
bulletin boards	pamphlets	supplements
classroom equipment	posters	supplies
collections	projects	technology
computers	reinforcement materials	videos
effective materials	related charts	visual aids
homework materials	school property	workbooks

30. MOTIVATING STUDENTS

a. Share your passion for learning with your students.

b. Provide each student with opportunities to experience success.

c. Encourage students to work toward meeting established goals.

d. Encourage students to (identify, realize, meet) goals equal to their potential.

e. Show students the link between school achievement and attaining lifetime goals.

f. Encourage students to apply themselves and to enjoy the challenges of (accomplishing tasks, attaining goals, improving skills, learning).

g. Demonstrate caring for students and show them you enjoy teaching them.

h. Highlight student work that exemplifies (growth, effort, quality).

i. Praise students for their efforts and accomplishments.

j. Motivate students by (giving positive feedback; making learning interesting, relevant, and fun; personalizing tasks and assignments; maintaining a healthy classroom culture; valuing every student) while enjoying teaching.

Vocabulary List

achievement	emphasize	opportunity
acknowledges	encouragement	problem solving
adjust	engage	realize
articulate	guide	reluctant
assist	high expectations	strategies
constructive	incorporate	support
displays	interact	supportive
effort	mechanics	visualize

31. MOTIVATING STUDENTS (PROFESSIONAL PRACTICES)

a. Consistently (offer, give) incentives for student achievement.

b. Promote achievement-oriented behaviors through engaging students in cooperative group activities.

c. Search for effective stimuli to pique student interests by using (Internet sites, professional journals, collaboration with colleagues, attendance at conventions/workshops).

d. Seek alternate methods of promoting student participation, including cooperative learning, physical activity, art, music, poetry, creative writing, role-playing, etc.

e. Encourage students to connect via e-mail with (institutions, individuals) around the globe for research and feedback.

f. Display student work (during, in) (open house, school/community events, common area display cases, commercial venues, libraries, etc.).

g. Relate subject matter to real-world situations to promote a greater understanding of (concepts, other people/cultures).

h. Plan (field trips, assemblies, demonstrations, guest presenters) to enhance students' interest.

i. Enter into partnerships with (museums, science centers, libraries, institutions of higher learning, agencies) to provide supplemental experiences.

j. (Become, Remain) (organized and prepared, enthusiastic, in possession of a range of appropriate and relevant material[s], open to discussion and feedback, eager to model expected outcomes/behaviors) and firm and fair.

Vocabulary List

assimilate	effective	plan
challenge	enhance	provide
creativity	experience	relevant
current	explore	share
desire	fact-filled	stress
devise	instill	student feelings
discovery	interesting	technology
display	opportunity	trends

32. MULTICULTURALISM

a. Include information regarding varied cultures through selective (choice, use) of materials that are relevant to all races, religions, and ethnicities.

b. Give students opportunities to form (partnerships, friendships, alliances) and to learn about other cultures through work in cooperative groups.

c. Embrace diversity, change, and inclusiveness.

d. Respect students' cultural differences.

e. Acknowledge the (needs, interests, concerns) of students representing different ethnic groups.

f. Help students recognize the cultural (needs, interests, concerns) of their fellow students.

g. Promote student interest in the cultural and artistic (influence, contribution) of others.

h. Increase student awareness of diverse cultures by promoting attendance at (festivals, exhibits, performances, workshops).

i. Learn the various (cultural traditions, family structures) of diverse student ethnicities.

j. Assist students arriving from other (cultures, schools, areas) in acclimating easily to (policies, language, routines) of the school/classroom by (providing policy manuals, meeting with their parents/guardians, assigning classroom buddies, communicating one-on-one, etc.).

Vocabulary List

adjustment	culture	rapport
adopt	demonstrate	respect
apply	differences	rules/standards
compromise	influence	self-esteem
concern	learning styles	temperament
contribution	mentor	uniqueness
counselor	mutual	value
cultural issues	nonjudgmental	viewpoint

33. NONINSTRUCTIONAL DUTIES

a. View performance of noninstructional duties as (essential, helpful, useful) to maintaining a school culture beneficial to the health, safety, and welfare of students.

b. Serve on planning committees for special school events.

c. Volunteer services to (PTA, parent council organization, community groups).

d. Report promptly for duty assignments and diligently perform tasks required to monitor (hall, lunchroom, bus, study hall, playground, field trip, community activities, fundraising projects).

e. (Develop, Maintain) a good rapport with the noninstructional personnel who perform school services.

f. Assist (community, social service, juvenile justice) groups engaged in programs to aid children.

g. Participate in fundraising activities held for school-related projects.

h. Support school (sporting, academic) events by attending when school is not in session.

i. Alert (security, guidance, administrative) staff to unusual/dangerous situations.

j. Perform noninstructional tasks willingly, exhibiting competence, grace, and professionalism.

Vocabulary List

advertise	direct	problem-solving
aid	distribute	records
announcements	edit	requests
assign duties	handle	schedules
complaints	inquires	sort
conduct	interviews	tasks
decision-making	liaison	transactions
details	maintain office	volunteer

34. NONTENURED TEACHER

a. Approach teaching with passion, energy, and humility.

b. (Become, Remain) (amenable, open) to replicating proven (methods, ideas) of planning to enhance teaching performance.

c. (Update, Compile) a (summative, professional) portfolio as supporting documentation of your (training, achievement, preparedness).

d. Draw on your (college, student teaching) experience to manage new challenges.

e. Engage in ongoing professional development through (distance learning, enrollment in degree programs, conferences, seminars, workshops).

f. Reflect on your teaching performance skills and (enhance, remediate) strategies where needed.

g. Brainstorm and network with (teacher-mentor, other nontenured staff, specialists) to obtain assistance.

h. Sustain a spirit of enthusiasm, commitment, and a strong desire to serve the needs of students.

i. (Build, Foster) a sound rapport with (school administrators, colleagues, students, parents, the community).

j. Identify areas of concern and implement a corrective action plan.

Vocabulary List

analyses	expectation	motivational techniques
anecdotal records	feeling tone	perform duties
assess	flexible	plan
communicate	hands-on	professionalism
concern	incorporate	record keeping
delivery	keep abreast of	understanding
effective	manipulative	viable
ethical	meticulous	well-maintained

35. ORGANIZATION

a. Set a personal example of (goal setting, planning, organization, preparedness) for students to emulate.

b. Build a professional portfolio that is comprehensive, organized, and aesthetically pleasing.

c. Organize and maintain (files, records, documentation, plans, reports, portfolios).

d. Develop effective methods to cope with (routine, specialized) responsibilities.

e. Organize classroom (materials, seating arrangement) in a manner that optimizes the classroom learning environment.

f. (Maintain, Keep) a comprehensive inventory of all classroom materials.

g. Organize lesson content to enhance instruction.

h. Organize and effectively manage students working in (cooperative groups, learning centers, individual cubicles, etc.).

i. Build and maintain a comprehensive, up-to-date substitute binder for a substitute teacher to use containing current lesson plans; generic plans/brain-twisters/puzzles; seating chart (with students' pictures); fire drill procedures; classroom rules and regulations; listing of bus, lunch, special subject, and bell schedules; attendance procedures; corridor passes; referral slips; listing of class helpers/jobs; locator notes for cabinet keys and electronic remotes; name/room number of helping teacher; and form for providing feedback.

j. Utilize computer software programs to facilitate organizing (files, supplies, student work, reports, etc.).

Vocabulary List

avoidance	materials available	regulate
collect	movement	reports
distribute	nonessential	roll book
elimination	orderly manner	routines
ensure	placement	safe
executed	plan book	smooth transition
irrelevant	prepared	storage
maintain	records	student preparation

36. PARENTS AS PARTNERS

a. (Maintain, Cultivate) a welcoming climate for parents.

b. Make (timely, constructive, purposeful) (written, telephone, e-mail) communication with parents and maintain an ongoing family-communication log.

c. Regularly inform parents of student progress.

d. Connect with parents through (visitations, writing letters, telephoning, e-mailing, sending text messages, attending conferences, attending meetings).

e. Alleviate parent anxieties through frequent communication concerning their child's progress.

f. Help parents recognize and understand the instructional methods and materials used with their child and offer (tips, training) on how they can (support, supplement) learning at home.

g. Advise parents on how to set up home-study areas for their child.

h. (Learn, Honor, Respect) cultural (customs, expectations) of parents.

i. Include parents as (volunteers, lecturers) to assist in the classroom.

j. Create a partnership alliance with parents.

Vocabulary List

accommodate	inquiry	positive attitude
admiration	interact	respect
advantage	involvement	supportive
cooperation	needs	tact
demonstrate	nurturing	understanding
discussion	open-mindedness	vision
facilitate	patience	visitation
fulfills	perspective	volunteers

37. PERSONAL ATTRIBUTES

a. Extend the school (preparation, work) day beyond the limits of the (opening, closing) schedule.

b. Infuse lessons with (tasteful, appropriate) (anecdotes, humor).

c. Become adept at adapting when required.

d. Begin each day with a renewed commitment to achieve goals.

e. Demonstrate the ability to overcome the challenges that teaching presents.

f. (Become, Remain) professional in personal appearance and conduct, serving as a model for students.

g. Demonstrate (conscientiousness, reliability, energy, industriousness, professionalism).

h. Practice (patience, empathy, consistency, fairness, firmness) when interacting with students.

i. Use correct and expressive spoken and written language.

j. Remain consistently professional in terms of personal habits and demeanor.

Vocabulary List

advocate	grace	professionalism
brainstorms	guides	remediation
counselor	initiatives	role-model
creative talent	modulated voice	serves
diagnosis	monitors	skills
dramatic	perform	speaking skills
efficient	pride	volunteer
friend	proctors	writing skills

38. PHYSICAL PLANT (CREATIVITY/AESTHETICS)

a. Maintain an experience-rich environment that engages students and motivates them to learn.

b. Maintain a neat and attractive classroom that is conducive to learning and to the well-being of the students.

c. Provide a literature-rich classroom environment.

d. Display student work.

e. Maintain a classroom environment that reflects best professional practices.

f. Display (charts, posters, hands-on projects) that reflect current (subjects, unit, themes) being taught.

g. Eradicate classroom clutter.

h. Display classroom visuals that reflect the (seasons of the year, course of study, unit, topic, subjects, current events).

i. Create (innovative, interactive) bulletin boards and workspaces that reflect the focus of curriculum study.

j. Partition (work, study, classroom) spaces into highly functional learning environments that support ease of learning and productive engagement of students.

Vocabulary List

aeration	displays	plan
arrange	diverse	prepare
cleanliness	efficient	productive
computers	equipment	provide
contribute	handle	safe
control	healthy	seating plan
custodial	maintain	technology
decorum	modification	transition

39. PHYSICAL PLANT (INSTRUCTIONAL SPACE)

a. Maintain the classroom as an emotional and physical safe haven and make (adaptations, accommodations) to students' environmental, sensory, and social stimulation needs to maximize student learning, including, but not exclusive to, providing (active/passive movement areas, elimination of physical and visual clutter, incorporation of appropriate music into the program, limiting the noise level, sustaining sound behavior management, providing instructional assistance, teaching to the learning styles and ability level of students, etc.).

b. Maintain an (appropriate, healthful) degree of (aeration, light) in the classroom.

c. Create work areas specific to program activities, including reading corners, quiet conversation centers, cooperative group area, multimedia center, technology center, etc.

d. Give students ready access to (charts, chalkboards, supplies, equipment, books).

e. Provide adequate storage space for consumable/nonconsumable (materials, equipment).

f. Require students to maintain their (workspace, desks, classroom, floor space) in a neat and orderly condition.

g. (Require, Encourage) students to share responsibility for maintaining the common areas in the classroom.

h. Make adaptations to the classroom environment to accommodate specific needs of students, including arranging a (quiet zone, stimuli-free areas, partitioned spaces, etc.).

i. Eliminate (safety, health) hazards.

j. Forward requests for classroom (repairs, maintenance, upkeep) to responsible building personnel.

Vocabulary List

aesthetics	maintenance	report deficiencies
bulletin boards	manage	respect
clean	manner	seating arrangements
condition	neat	standards
consistent	orderly manner	sufficient
consumable materials	organize	supplies
displays	ownership	textbooks
maintain	repairs	well-maintained

40. PLANNING (LESSON PLANS)

a. Plan extensively to meet the (curriculum requirements, varied needs) of the students.

b. (Follow, Meet) mandated guidelines as to (organization, content, clarity, professional quality, comprehensiveness, frequency) of lesson plans.

c. Formulate student-centered plans that reflect (school, district) mandates as well as sound professional pedagogy.

d. Write lesson plans that are aligned with (curriculum guides, grade, school mandates, district mandates, core standards, student Individualized Education Plans).

e. Develop an awareness of how children learn and include effective teaching strategies in lesson activities.

f. Plan activities that are appropriate for the (developmental, academic, learning) (level/style) of the students.

g. Highlight focus area(s) in the plan book to promote clarity and emphasis.

h. Integrate (basic skills, test-taking skills, technology, audiovisuals) into plans.

i. (Upgrade, Maintain) the (content, clarity, neatness, quality, comprehensiveness) of the lesson plans as required.

j. Display an interdisciplinary approach to instructional delivery in the lesson plans.

Vocabulary List

adhere	current events	objectives
align	curriculum content	preparation
alternatives	hands-on	proficiency
appropriate	information	relevant
A/V equipment	innovative	require
child-centered	learning centers	supplementary
conform	manipulative	technology
core standards	mastery	variety

41. PREPARATION FOR DELIVERY OF INSTRUCTION (TEACHER)

a. (Maintain, Collect, Use) a repertoire of (ice-breaking, energizing, hook) opening (exercises, activities) to promote student readiness for learning.

b. (Review, Solve, Examine) all (assignments, material) before (use, delivery of instruction).

c. Leave (room, opportunity) for (questions, discussion, demonstration, group activities) when planning.

d. Prepare and deliver a concise, cogent message.

e. Vary lesson components to engage the (interest, senses) of students of diverse (learning styles, interest/ability levels, knowledge bases).

f. (Plan, Allow room) for (creativity, problem solving, critical thinking, feedback) (in, from) the students.

g. (Develop, Gain) a comprehensive knowledge of (subject matter, the curriculum).

h. (Develop, Perfect) a presentation style that captures and engages student interest.

i. Become able to handle (interruptions, the unexpected) with grace and competence.

j. Conduct a brief and substantive review of prior learning before (offering, presenting, modeling) new (information, material, assignments).

Vocabulary List

address	concise	improvement
administer	consequences	interest
alter	consistent	modify
anticipate	dependable	observation
appearance	developmental needs	prepare
avoid	differentiate	revision
climate	expertise	solution
competence	implement	strive

42. PREPARATION FOR LEARNING (STUDENTS)

a. Use an expansive (technology-enhanced, multimedia, audiovisual) anticipatory set activity to (introduce, set the tone for, overview, heighten interest in) (unit, theme-based) study for the lesson.

b. Use a (hook activity, tangible teaching aid, demonstration) to stimulate (interest in, readiness for) the topic to be discussed.

c. Start (the, each) lesson by conducting a (review of prior learning, discussion, experiment, activity) related to the topic.

d. Discuss lesson objectives and expected outcomes with students prior to introducing next (phase of lesson, activity, component of the lesson).

e. Consistently model expected behavior.

f. Communicate expectations for learning.

g. Conduct opening activities that establish a framework for presenting new (topics, skills).

h. Align (lesson, learning) objectives with assessment piece when (writing, constructing) the lesson plan.

i. Conduct an extended and comprehensive set activity when introducing (unit-themed study) units, including (guest speakers, photography, audiovisual, art, journaling, exhibits, field trips, Powerpoint presentations, literature, etc.).

j. Conduct set activities that are participatory, concise, and highly relevant.

Vocabulary List

ability	direct	maximize
achieve	effectiveness	monitor
awareness	encourage	on-going
clarify	enhance	opportunity
climate	establish	outcomes
communicate	expectation	plan
conducive	gear	question
demeanor	indirect	techniques

43. PROBLEM-BASED LEARNING (PBL)

a. (Develop, Build) competency in structuring effective problem-based learning activities after engaging in appropriate professional development.

b. Design relevant, thought-provoking problems.

c. Allow students to (practice, learn, work through) problems that provide a framework of skills in preparation for successfully solving challenges of the (real world, global community, continuing education).

d. (Integrate, Offer) problem-based learning as a part of a comprehensive array of teaching/learning strategies.

e. Successfully utilize (creativity, flexibility) in (managing, scheduling, structuring) (time, resources, support personnel) during problem-based learning activities.

f. (Be willing to, Grow comfortable with) (give, giving) students greater independence to (succeed, fail, manage time, rework, discover solutions) when engaging in problem-based learning activities.

g. Support student endeavors during problem-based learning by providing appropriate (coaching, mentoring, support, encouragement).

h. Provide students with complete (long-term, comprehensive) training in the problem-based learning process before having them engage in the program.

i. (Lead, Direct) students to review group interaction (skills, experiences) previously used during cooperative learning activities (when, before) embarking on problem-based learning activities.

j. Become competent in the use of (appropriate, effective) (material, strategies, questioning techniques) required in managing problem-based learning.

Vocabulary List

ability	focus	research
adjust	forum	resolution
constructive	goals	re-teach
cooperative learning	group work	routine
demonstrate	mastery	strategies
design	motivate	study habits
discussion	proficiency	styles
feedback	promote	sufficient time

44. PROFESSIONAL DEVELOPMENT

a. (Work toward meeting, Earn) NCLB professional standard of "highly qualified."

b. (Review, Become knowledgeable of) current best practices research.

c. Strengthen teaching proficiencies through the use of (technology, laboratory projects, best practice research, professional journals, related software, post graduate courses, conferences/workshops, videoconferences, distance learning, summer academies).

d. Demonstrate the ability to assimilate and implement educational reform (techniques, mandates, methods, programs).

e. Keep up with educational trends and advancements so that (personal knowledge, professional ability) remains current.

f. Examine alternative teaching practices by visiting (out-of-district school sites, colleges, laboratory schools, charter schools).

g. Purchase or access (professional journals, periodicals, a professional book club membership, computer software) to keep abreast of contemporary issues in education.

h. Attend professional (workshops, seminars, conventions, symposiums, inservice sessions, continuing education courses) to remain current with educational trends.

i. Enroll in (evening classes, weekend classes, distance learning courses, summer institutes, telecourses) to further professional growth.

j. Network with (institutes of higher learning, teacher training centers, colleagues, professional groups) to enhance professional knowledge.

Vocabulary List

character	enthusiastic	plan
community	implement	self-analytical
conduct	journal	self-reflective
constructive	knowledgeable	strive
current issues	opportunity	sustain
decision-making	participate	texts
demonstrate	peer review	use
display	periodicals	vitality

45. PROFESSIONAL HABITS (PERSONAL)

a. Ensure that the passion for (learning, teaching) is evident—and contagious.

b. Allow constructive suggestions to result in (reflection, solutions, renewed effort).

c. Demonstrate the (behaviors, values) expected of students, including (trust, diligence, selflessness, cooperation, caring, patience, perseverance, etc.).

d. View challenges as opportunities to (excel, try harder).

e. Maintain a (professional, excellent) (appearance, record of attendance/promptness, demeanor).

f. (Remain, Become) cooperative and agreeable and (build, enjoy) a sound rapport with (administration, colleagues, parents).

g. Show enthusiasm for teaching.

h. (Become, Remain) consistent, reliable, cooperative, and competent in the performance of (instructional, noninstructional) duties.

i. Exhibit energy and enthusiasm in completing assignments.

j. (Become, Remain) dedicated in the desire to make a positive change in the lives of students and to ensure that their educational experiences are those of productivity and joy.

Vocabulary List

analyzes	discipline	partnerships
apprenticeship	flexible	prepared
avert	follow	provide
cogent	imaginative	school-based activities
competent	innovative	special projects
constructive	interpret	support
cooperative	knowledgeable	training programs
creative	maximize	works

46. PROFESSIONAL HABITS (WORKPLACE)

a. Ensure that the classroom environment embodies (a culture of success, creativity, caring and cooperation, a true learning environment).

b. (Become, Remain) flexible and receptive to the use of new (ideas, techniques, materials, methods, requirements, technology).

c. Follow (programs, projects) through to their logical conclusion.

d. Willingly share (ideas, materials, responsibilities, expertise) with colleagues.

e. Work effectively, both independently and collaboratively.

f. Hold high expectations for (personal, student) achievement.

g. Support the school (mission, vision, goal).

h. Remain up-to-date with teaching techniques.

i. Work toward earning an (advanced degree, additional certification) via (distance, online, graduate school) venues.

j. Keep abreast of new developments relating to (subject area, grade level, curriculum, program, profession).

Vocabulary List

aesthetic	current	provide
arrange	ensure	repair
attention	environment	resource
cleanliness	maintenance	seating arrangements
coalesce	manage	standards
consistent	organize	sufficiency
construct	ownership	supplies
creative	productive	tidy

47. RAPPORT WITH STUDENTS

    a. (Respect, Consider) the students' points of view.

    b. Become energized through interaction with students.

    c. (Connect with, Empower) students by showing a personal interest in their (interests, concerns).

    d. Relate to students in a manner that promotes trust and mutual respect.

    e. Demonstrate an interest in students, both individually and collectively.

    f. Build a positive rapport with students through giving/asking for feedback, encouraging, acting as a role model and counselor, remaining consistent and fair in treatment, giving and requiring respect, and caring enough to be the best.

    g. Demonstrate optimism, confidence, and hope when interacting with students.

    h. Be firm but fair.

    i. Encourage positive exchanges between students.

    j. Make every effort to find qualities in each student that can be nurtured and celebrated.

Vocabulary List

attitude	disciplinary	opportunity
avert	enforcer	order
behavior modification	firm but fair	organization
compromise	influence	rapport
concern	inspirational	recourse
culture	learning styles	respect
demonstrate	manner	safety
develop	nonjudgmental	temperament

48. RECORD KEEPING

a. Maintain a well-documented, updated professional portfolio supported by descriptive artifacts.

b. Use appropriate software to (track, assess, record, manage) student (progress, grades, discipline referrals, attendance) (records, reports).

c. Keep a comprehensive roll book that reflects (student progress, grades, homework/project completion, anecdotal records).

d. Maintain accurate (semester, term, marking period, annual, portfolio) records.

e. Maintain records according to (school, district) guidelines.

f. Reply promptly to requests for professional data.

g. (Refer to, Preserve) (school, district) memorandums for compliance and/or future reference.

h. Keep a record of (contact with parents, professional development activities).

i. Maintain a planbook that reflects (flexible planning, pacing of lesson content, core curriculum standards, textbooks, manipulatives, materials, tests) and that clearly (delineates, highlights) (segments requiring review, indicators of completed work, revisions and adjustments, special events, medical memorandums).

j. Support (grades, referrals) given by maintaining a comprehensive, ongoing record of assessment data, including summative test results, record of completion of (assignments, tasks), behavior referrals, attendance, anecdotal records, journal entries.

Vocabulary List

adjustments	current	participation
alternate planning	evaluate	performance
assign	evidence	portfolio
compliance	failure	preparation
comprehensive	goals	quality
comprehensiveness	growth	record
construct	innovation	thorough
copious	maintain	up-to-date

49. REFLECTION

a. (Encourage, Engage in, Initiate) growth-producing conversations with (administrators, supervisory personnel, colleagues, mentors) to gain (insight, perspective) on teaching performance.

b. (Recognize, Value) varied (approaches, points of view) to reaching (consensus, solutions).

c. Develop (self-assessment, reflective analysis) skills and routinely evaluate your professional performance.

d. Remain open to constructive suggestions.

e. Effectively (review, reflect on) the delivery of instruction to help further (positive outcomes, student achievement, professional growth, administrative suggestions, action plan objectives).

f. Acknowledge accountability for student outcomes.

g. Set rigorous personal performance standards.

h. Develop improvement plans based on prior performance assessments, self-analysis, and through collaboration with evaluators.

i. Implement and develop (strategies, projects, activities) to show that planned improvements have been realized.

j. Direct an ongoing evaluation of effectiveness via (student outcomes, attainment of objectives, feedback from observations and/or evaluations).

Vocabulary List

admire	maturity	respects
communicate	mentor	role-model
contribute	open-minded	tact
explain	perspective	talent
friendly	positive attitude	vision
gifted	productive	volunteer
grace	professional	wholesome
interact	rapport	work habits

50. RELATIONSHIPS WITH COLLEAGUES

a. Enjoy a feeling of camaraderie and sense of belonging during group interaction.

b. Enjoy a shared sense of purpose through collaborative interaction.

c. Credit others by attributing successful outcomes to combined (skills, input, effort) as the result of collective group endeavor.

d. Cultivate warm professional relationships with colleagues.

e. (Establish a sound rapport, Cooperate) with agencies that interact with (students, parents, the school).

f. Help with (grade-level, school, community) projects and (remain, become) committed to the (goals, programs, mission) of the school.

g. Interact with (specialists, teacher assistants, aides, paraeducators) to enhance opportunities for student (achievement, activities).

h. Work effectively and productively with (administrator, support staff, specialists, ESL/bilingual staff, child study team, etc.) to enhance student success.

i. Sustain sound relationships with (facilitators, substitute teachers, staff developers, aides, team/department leaders, administrators).

j. Willingly share (ideas, materials, expertise, responsibilities) with colleagues.

Vocabulary List

accept	initiative	responsible
adept	input	share
analytical	leadership	strive
assist	manner	support
collegiality	participate	volunteer
decision-making	professional	welfare
engage	rapport	willing
importance	reflective	work

51. RELATIONSHIPS WITH PARENTS AND COMMUNITY

a. Make a special effort to (accommodate, include) (foster parents, grandparents, guardians, senior citizens, volunteers) in the classroom culture.

b. Inform parents (frequently, often, weekly, monthly) of their children's progress.

c. Encourage and value parental input and decision-making capabilities regarding children's learning experiences.

d. Respect and gain knowledge about the various cultures represented in the (school, community).

e. (Learn about, Make referrals to) available community resources that might aid students and their families.

f. Create a parent-friendly atmosphere within the classroom.

g. Utilize (e-mail, telephone, written notes) to communicate with parents.

h. Organize with (social service agencies, public safety units, community groups, corporations) to promote student-based initiatives.

i. Prepare and present folders to parents at the beginning of the school year that include a map of the school, (telephone number, e-mail address) for communication, school code of conduct, curriculum objectives for the grade level, assessment mandates (standardized tests), classroom rules and regulations, attendance mandates, available school resource personnel, visitation rules, report card content, and dates of distribution.

j. Network with students and families through community involvement.

Vocabulary List

clarify	facilitate	probe
comprehend	feedback	progress
cooperation	insight	question
creative	inspire	recognition
effectiveness	interest	request
effort	knowledge	support
enhance	maintain	understand
experiential	multicultural	utilize

52. SCHOOL CULTURE (SCHOOL CLIMATE)

a. Act decisively and effectively to protect students against (negative, harmful) (experiences, interactions) with others, including (bullying, threats, acts of intolerance, abuse, harassment, racism, sexism, etc.).

b. Enforce school (rules, code of conduct) consistently and fairly.

c. Establish and maintain a safe and caring classroom environment.

d. Uphold (school, district, mandated) rules and regulations.

e. (Review, Explain) the school code of conduct (for, to) students and their parents.

f. Maintain a classroom environment that inspires students to (reach for, attain) academic success.

g. Contribute to school initiatives designed to enhance the (school, classroom) climate, thereby becoming empowered to make suggestions for improvement.

h. Make every effort to ensure that the overall school climate remains positive.

i. Preserve a safe environment to ensure student (physical, emotional, personal) well-being.

j. Generate a healthy and productive social and emotional relationship with students by (connecting curriculum to students' lives and culture, treating students as valued individuals, providing authentic learning experiences, encouraging inquiry, engaging in meaningful discussion, maintaining a sound learning environment, etc.).

Vocabulary List

behaviors	counseling	intervention
channel	debate	modification
collective	demonstrate	procedure
conducive	dialogue	responsible
consult	encourage	social interaction
control	evaluate	standard
cope	implement	technique
correct	indicate	test

53. SELF-ESTEEM (STUDENTS)

a. Encourage students to be their "own best friends."

b. (Build in, Point out) personal relevancy of subject matter to students' (culture, ethnicity, frame of reference).

c. Build self-confidence in students through facilitating their productive (participation in, contribution to) group activities.

d. (Encourage, Build) student self-esteem and sensitivity to the feelings of others.

e. Recognize and validate students' (contributions, feelings, ideas).

f. Embrace the unique qualities of each student.

g. Encourage students to participate actively in class and interact positively with others.

h. (Become, Remain) sensitive to the (emotional needs, family concerns) of the students.

i. (Become, Remain) nonjudgmental in interacting with students and strive to respect their points of view.

j. Demonstrate through actions that each student is important and each student's input matters.

Vocabulary List

acceptance	feelings	respect
collaboration	generous	sensitive
define	incentive	solicit
diversity	incorporate	suggestion
emotional	insights	support
empower	patience	thoughts
exhibit	positive	tolerance
fairness	recognize	validate

54. SELF-MOTIVATION (STUDENTS)

a. Allow students to experience failure—without fault.

b. Motivate students to (achieve, contribute) through their interaction with others in (cooperative, problem-based) learning groups.

c. Encourage students to participate fully in (classroom, extracurricular, sports, academic, cultural, group) activities.

d. Provide students with a range of activities that affords them the best opportunity for success.

e. Allow students to choose among a variety of learning experiences, including (interest-based mini-lessons, learning center activities, hands-on activities, peer partners, independent research, exper- imentation, computer-assisted learning).

f. Hold students to rigorous standards of achievement.

g. Avert negative interactions between students regarding their (ability, progress, potential, grades, disabilities, weaknesses) and promote a climate of acceptance, compassion, and enlightened interaction.

h. Encourage students' curiosity.

i. Encourage students to become independent learners by giving and receiving feedback on progress, individualizing (assignments, tasks), maintaining a nurturing learning environment, valuing contributions and input, and providing incentives for learning.

j. Encourage students to be leaders.

Vocabulary List

adopt	excel	performance
attention	excellence	potential
build	fair	praise
concerns	fears	problems
cooperation	growth	recognition
demeanor	insecurities	self-worth
effect	motivation	special needs
effort	participate	support

55. SPECIAL NEEDS (SPECIAL EDUCATION)

a. Effectively (plan, work) with (traditional education, inclusion, paraeducator) (partners, teachers, aides) to serve needs of traditional and special needs students.

b. Use cooperative learning group (behaviors, activities) as (instruments, strategies) beneficial to promoting (friendships, alliances, understanding) of (mainstreamed, special needs) students.

c. (Become, Remain) sensitive to sensory processing (limitations, constraints) of (inclusion, mainstream) students when posting visual displays.

d. (Become, Remain) proficient in working with special education (rules, regulations, legislation, time lines, guidelines, programs, personnel).

e. (Understand, Become conversant with) (inclusion, mainstreaming) programs and precepts and work effectively with students in the program.

f. Make adaptations to plans and delivery of instruction to accommodate the needs of (inclusion, mainstream) students, inclusive of, but not limited to, complexity of assignments, time allotted for completion of assignments, increased use of concrete aids, increased level of extra support, use of verbal cues, use of varied assessment modalities, etc.

g. (Become conversant with, Know) the content of the Individualized Education Plans (IEPs) of all students in the (special education, inclusion, mainstream, prevention, intervention) program.

h. Provide access to both the general curriculum and extracurricular activities for special needs students.

i. (Become, Remain) sensitive to the specific (developmental, physical, social, instructional, emotional) needs of special needs students.

j. Work productively with (crisis intervention staff, the child study team, special education staff, the guidance counselor, parents, administrators) to coordinate needed student services.

Vocabulary List

achieve	cooperative	interest
adjust	critical thinking	measure
assistance	encourage	monitor
awareness	engage	order
benefit	exceed	outcome
climate	feedback	prompt
communicate	focus	question
contribute	implement	stimulate

56. STANDARDS AND PRACTICES

a. Use the core curriculum standards as the foundation for (planning, delivery of instruction).

b. Weave universal (character-building, value-based) themes into lessons, including (peaceful coexistence, respect for self and others, discipline and self-control, appropriate behavior and appearance, honesty, truthfulness, etc.) where appropriate.

c. Require students to use proper grammar and to write (neatly, clearly, correctly).

d. Routinely incorporate basic skills into lessons.

e. Uphold and enforce the (school mission, school policy).

f. Encourage students to (be cooperative, be personable, be team players, clearly enunciate).

g. Require students to practice good (organization, time management, note-taking, communication, listening) skills.

h. Provide challenging and rewarding educational experiences for all students.

i. Ensure, through professional expertise, that students receive high-quality instruction in areas cited by national, district, and school policies.

j. Promptly and effectively comply with all (school, district, state) mandates.

Vocabulary List

adhere	follow	pilot
appropriate	formulate	prerequisite
build	foundation	prescribe
consistent	guide	proficient
content	lesson objective	requirements
curriculum	mandate	routine
decency	methods	teach
enforce	participate	upheld

57. STUDENT BEHAVIORS

a. Keep students engaged and focused by providing prepared supplementary activity kits for students who finish tasks quickly.

b. Teach students to respond promptly and appropriately to (signaled, verbal, audible) cues.

c. Anticipate and deflect student off-task behaviors.

d. Utilize (mediation, tact, understanding, patience, empathy, logic, wisdom, expertise) to remedy classroom behavior problems.

e. Involve students in the process of establishing classroom (rules, code of conduct) and in monitoring the effectiveness of classroom rules.

f. (Promote, Reward) student self-control, cooperation, and productivity.

g. Help students to develop peer mediation skills and use them effectively to resolve conflict.

h. Hold students (accountable, responsible) for the consequences brought about as a result of their off-task actions.

i. Act proactively to detect, report, and eliminate (bullying, aggressive, offensive, threatening, suicidal) student behavior.

j. Hold students (responsible, accountable) for remaining current with their educational (program, assignments) in the event (in-school, out-of-school) (suspension, expulsion) is imposed.

Vocabulary List

afford	expectation	purpose
anticipatory	experiences	recall
communicate	explain	relate
construct	feelings	scope
definition	involve	skill
description	model	synopsis
discussion	objective	tasks
employ	personal	transfer

58. STUDENTS FIRST

a. Delight in moments when students "get it."

b. (Find, Celebrate) the positive qualities in each student.

c. Continuously help students on a(n) (individual, group) basis.

d. Acknowledge (social, emotional, cultural) needs and interests of the students.

e. Remain open and responsive to student needs.

f. Strive to meet the needs of all students.

g. Remain aware of (social, emotional, cultural, economic, familial) factors that impact students.

h. Focus on the development and education of the whole child.

i. Seek ways to impact the lives of students positively.

j. (Display, Demonstrate) a belief and a dedication to the premise that all children can learn.

Vocabulary List

ability	effective	motivate
age	explore	opportunity
assimilate	feelings	process
challenge	information	resources
clear	instill	share
creativity	involve	stress
desire	master	trends
display	materials	understand

59. SUPPLEMENTAL PRACTICES

a. Utilize selective Web sites to obtain (creative, useful) (practice, supplemental) (lesson plans, exercises, activities).

b. (Involve, Work with) students (in, during) (afterschool, lunchtime) activities.

c. Encourage student involvement in (school, city, regional, state, national) competitions.

d. Assist students to (prepare, research, build, design) competition entries.

e. Volunteer (expertise, special talents, assistance) to the (school, community) where needed.

f. Support student involvement in (extracurricular, social, athletic, educational) activities.

g. Serve as a school resource.

h. Provide personal recommendations when requested.

i. Embrace a positive personal philosophy regarding (teaching, children, learning).

j. Serve as (advisor, tutor, mentor, facilitator, coach) to benefit and support student endeavors.

Vocabulary List

available	execute	prepare
avoidance	extraneous	regulate
collect	irrelevant	relevant
delineate	manage	require
distribute	manner	routine
elimination	nonessential	specific
enhance	orderly	storage
ensure	placement	submit

60. SUPPORTING STUDENTS

a. (Become, Remain) alert and proactive in intervening in situations involving students' (psychological, behavioral, emotional, social, physical) well-being.

b. Assess student aptitudes and assess progress in the light of their (abilities, scores, interests, learning styles).

c. Regroup students and differentiate instruction according to academic need.

d. Conduct ongoing summative assessments and modify instruction accordingly.

e. Provide opportunities for students to demonstrate achievement through a variety of methods.

f. Evaluate student work promptly and equitably.

g. Encourage students to strive for (improvement, excellence, greater achievement).

h. Conduct assessments and use test results to facilitate (reteaching, remediation, enrichment) efforts.

i. Support students' efforts to earn (honor society memberships, awards, scholarships, grants, fellowships, certificates of achievement).

j. Poll students as to (what they like/enjoy about school, what they would change, what they dislike) and honor their responses.

Vocabulary List

adjustment	document	objective
administer	efficient	practical
aid	emulate	quality
alternate	gear	reflective
articulate	improvement	review
competencies	innovative	stimulate
conduct	interdisciplinary	support
difficulty	model	variety

61. TEACHER AS MENTOR

a. (Teach, Infuse) (life lessons, life skills) for students' future engagement (at the next academic level, in the community, in the world, with the curriculum).

b. Take students struggling with (academic, behavioral, personal) difficulties under your wing.

c. Share professional experiences and teaching expertise with (colleagues, student teachers, professional development staff, aides, assistants, paraeducators).

d. (Volunteer, Maintain) the classroom as a laboratory in which best teaching practices can be observed.

e. Support initiatives to raise levels of teaching performance by working toward (lead, master, head) teacher designation to qualify to serve in that capacity.

f. Display and share strong organizational skills and classroom management techniques with (student teachers, teaching assistants, classroom aides, paraeducators).

g. (Earn, Work toward qualifying for) (grants, awards, honors, certificates, honorariums, testimonials, recognition) for professional achievement.

h. Volunteer as a student advisor.

i. Engage and host guest speakers.

j. (Willingly, Effectively) (demonstrate to, accommodate, coach) student teachers (in a, a) range of teaching experiences that exhibits best professional practices.

Vocabulary List

allow	focus	provide
constructive	incorporate	relative
demonstration	mechanics	remedial
design	motivate	research
direct	ongoing	resolution
encourage	prior	style
expect	problems	
feedback	promote	

62. TECHNOLOGY (PROFESSIONAL USE)

a. Serve as a turnkey facilitator for colleagues after (advanced training, ongoing development) in the use of technology in the classroom.

b. Use the Internet to (connect, network, videoconference) with (experts, specialists, colleagues, parents, interest groups) and share information relative to (best teaching practices, educational trends, topics of mutual interest).

c. Explore technological advances as they relate to the students' (grade level, curriculum, learning styles).

d. Integrate technology into instruction in the content areas to support student learning and development of higher-order thinking skills.

e. Build upon (analytical, research, teaching) skills by gaining proficiency with advanced technology.

f. Develop (e-mail, distance learning, bookmarking, up/downloading, Web site development, podcasting) capabilities.

g. (Remain, Become) proficient in the use of computer-assisted instruction techniques, including the use of (graphics, multimedia, PowerPoint presentations, discussion forums).

h. Provide computerized instruction (in addition to, to enhance) traditional methods.

i. Participate in (district, college, online, distance learning) workshops to (upgrade, keep abreast of) technical skills and knowledge basic to current educational demands.

j. Keep current in the knowledge and use of technological advances to (meet student needs, meet professional demands, enhance professionalism, gain increased respect of students).

Vocabulary List

appropriate	experience	opportunity
committee	experimentation	optimal
connect	gather	real-world
contemporary	global	relevant
current	information	supplement
delivery	instruction	technique
development	integrate	train
enhance	involvement	travel

63. TECHNOLOGY (STUDENT-CENTERED)

a. (Warn, Enlighten) students concerning the (realities, pitfalls, benefits) of (electronic messaging, chat rooms, video/photo uploading/downloading, blogs, cyberspace, etc.).

b. (Encourage, Assist) parents to understand the (impact, benefits) of technology as a learning tool.

c. Teach students to be safe consumers of cyberspace.

d. Preview and monitor all student (Internet, cyberspace, social-networking, CD-ROM, DVD) activities.

e. Assign appropriate software for students to (research, practice, review, assess) assignments independently.

f. (Remain, Become) (conversant with, knowledgeable of) student "techno-speak" in terms of their use of (e-mail, text/instant messaging, blogs).

g. Incorporate (interactive, multimedia) technology into traditional instruction.

h. Utilize specialized software programs to enhance (classroom activities, record-keeping capabilities).

i. Monitor the use and assess the value of student work with (computers, Web sites, the Internet, e-mail, video games, CDs, DVDs, videos).

j. Encourage students to collaborate in their use of personal computers.

Vocabulary List

afford	discovery	instill
approach	effective	interest
A/V materials	enjoy	resources
challenge	environment	strategies
concept	experience	support
definition	explores	transfer
desire	fact-filled	unique
devise	information	vary

64. TEST-TAKING SKILLS

a. (Facilitate, Help, Assist) students needing extra support to work with (tutors, peers, parents, online tutorial sites, off-site agencies, morning/afterschool programs, test-prep classes) on test preparation activities.

b. Familiarize students with topics that will be covered on the test.

c. Integrate test-taking strategies during classroom instruction in the basic content areas.

d. Adequately prepare students for (proficiency, achievement, unit, midterm, final, standardized, advanced placement, etc.) exams.

e. Recognize the (factors, attitudes, anxieties, experiences) that negatively impact students' performance on tests and conduct (conversations, exercises) to (eliminate, defuse) their (impact, influence).

f. Enhance the opportunity for students' successful performance on tests by providing (study books, tutoring, practice tests, specialized software, stress reduction techniques, content reviews).

g. Interpret test results for (students, parents, specialists) to provide (services, material, aid) available to them and use data to refine the curriculum and the delivery of instruction.

h. Explain (relevance, scores, meaning) of student test results and (teach, advise) them how to put test taking into the proper perspective.

i. Supply information on (relaxation techniques, focus techniques, test structure, timed responses, feelings of self-empowerment, adopting positive attitudes) to help improve students' test performance.

j. Help students (understand, utilize) principles of (studying, internalizing information), including, but not limited to, (making material meaningful, building on prior knowledge, organizing facts, reciting information in own words, forming mental pictures, taking notes, making and reviewing lists, maintaining a positive attitude, practicing, studying with a partner/group, anticipating success).

Vocabulary List

accept	constructs	mechanics
accurate	criterion-reference	monitors
achievement	effectiveness	non-traditional
administers	elicits	problem-solving
alternative	employ	response
assessment	encourages	review
comprehension	entertain	self-assessment
conducts	evaluation	utilizes

65. TIME MANAGEMENT

a. Conduct (expeditious, smooth) transitions between (lessons, class periods, curriculum segments).

b. Maximize instructional time by effectively (prioritizing tasks, organizing data, preparing materials, enlisting assistance, delegating tasks, scheduling free time, using flexible planning).

c. Teach mini-lessons and give timely (closure, reflection, review, feedback, reteaching) when needed.

d. Eliminate classroom distractions.

e. Allow sufficient time to complete (closure activities, assessments, recording of homework assignments, note taking, discussion).

f. Stress the importance of productively utilizing class time to students.

g. Plan creative and productive ways to utilize class time (block scheduling, double periods) to enhance the learning experience.

h. Promptly (deliver, pick up) class for special subject (periods, classes).

i. Utilize preparation periods for school-related activities.

j. Arrange classroom workspace for easy access to (supplies, equipment, files, personal effects).

Vocabulary List

accurate	maintain	require
anticipate	organize	review
available	performance	schedule
comprehensive	periodic	submits
ensure	plan	time frame
establish	preparation	timelessness
experience	prepare	timely
goals	progress	up-to-date

PART II

The Improvement Plan Packet With Reproducible Forms

PERFORMANCE PROGRESS AND IMPROVEMENT PLAN

Teacher: _____ **School:** _____ **Page 1**

Grade/Department: _____

PART ONE: ANALYSIS OF TEACHER PERFORMANCE

65 PROFICIENCY CATEGORIES

☐ 1. Accountability

☐ 2. Administration

☐ 3. Affective Domain

☐ 4. Assessment

☐ 5. Behavior Modification

☐ 6. Brain-Based Learning

☐ 7. Clarity

☐ 8. Closure

☐ 9. Collaboration

☐ 10. Cooperative Learning

☐ 11. Creativity

☐ 12. Critical Thinking

☐ 13. Curriculum Delivery

☐ 14. Curriculum Knowledge (Knowledge of Content)

☐ 15. Curriculum Management

☐ 16. Discipline (Classroom Management)

☐ 17. Evaluation

☐ 18. Extracurricular Activities

☐ 19. Feedback to Students

☐ 20. Goal Setting for Students

☐ 21. Guidance

☐ 22. Instructional Delivery

☐ 23. Instructional Diversity

☐ 24. Leadership Skills

☐ 25. Learning Styles (Multiple Intelligences)

☐ 26. Lesson Objectives

☐ 27. Managing Academic Diversity

☐ 28. Mandated Programs

☐ 29. Materials

☐ 30. Motivating Students

☐ 31. Motivating Students (Professional Practices)

☐ 32. Multiculturalism

☐ 33. Noninstructional Duties

☐ 34. Nontenured Teacher

☐ 35. Organization

☐ 36. Parents as Partners

☐ 37. Personal Attributes

☐ 38. Physical Plant (Creativity/Aesthetics)

☐ 39. Physical Plant (Instructional Space)

☐ 40. Planning (Lesson Plans)

☐ 41. Preparation for Delivery of Instruction

☐ 42. Preparation for Learning

☐ 43. Problem-Based Learning

☐ 44. Professional Development

☐ 45. Professional Habits (Personal)

☐ 46. Professional Habits (Workplace)

☐ 47. Rapport With Students

☐ 48. Record Keeping

☐ 49. Reflection

☐ 50. Relationships With Colleagues

☐ 51. Relationships With Parents and Community

☐ 52. School Culture

☐ 53. Self-Esteem (Students)

☐ 54. Self-Motivation (Students)

☐ 55. Special Needs (Special Education)

☐ 56. Standards and Practices

☐ 57. Student Behaviors

☐ 58. Students First

☐ 59. Supplemental Practices

☐ 60. Supporting Students

☐ 61. Teacher as Mentor

☐ 62. Technology (Professional Use)

☐ 63. Technology (Student Centered)

☐ 64. Test-Taking Skills

☐ 65. Time Management

TEACHER STRENGTHS					
AREAS NEEDING IMPROVEMENT					
SUGGESTIONS FOR IMPROVEMENT					

EVALUATEE'S SIGNATURE: _____

EVALUATOR'S SIGNATURE: _____ **DATE:** ____/____/_____

PERFORMANCE PROGRESS AND IMPROVEMENT PLAN

Teacher: _____   School: _____   **Page 2**

Grade/Department: _____

PART TWO: TEACHER SELF-ASSESSMENT FORM

65 PROFICIENCY CATEGORIES

☐ 1. Accountability
☐ 2. Administration
☐ 3. Affective Domain
☐ 4. Assessment
☐ 5. Behavior Modification
☐ 6. Brain-Based Learning
☐ 7. Clarity
☐ 8. Closure
☐ 9. Collaboration
☐ 10. Cooperative Learning
☐ 11. Creativity
☐ 12. Critical Thinking
☐ 13. Curriculum Delivery
☐ 14. Curriculum Knowledge (Knowledge of Content)
☐ 15. Curriculum Management
☐ 16. Discipline (Classroom Management)
☐ 17. Evaluation
☐ 18. Extracurricular Activities
☐ 19. Feedback to Students
☐ 20. Goal Setting for Students
☐ 21. Guidance
☐ 22. Instructional Delivery
☐ 23. Instructional Diversity

☐ 24. Leadership Skills
☐ 25. Learning Styles (Multiple Intelligences)
☐ 26. Lesson Objectives
☐ 27. Managing Academic Diversity
☐ 28. Mandated Programs
☐ 29. Materials
☐ 30. Motivating Students
☐ 31. Motivating Students (Professional Practices)
☐ 32. Multiculturalism
☐ 33. Noninstructional Duties
☐ 34. Nontenured Teacher
☐ 35. Organization
☐ 36. Parents as Partners
☐ 37. Personal Attributes
☐ 38. Physical Plant (Creativity/Aesthetics)
☐ 39. Physical Plant (Instructional Space)
☐ 40. Planning (Lesson Plans)
☐ 41. Preparation for Delivery of Instruction
☐ 42. Preparation for Learning
☐ 43. Problem-Based Learning

☐ 44. Professional Development
☐ 45. Professional Habits (Personal)
☐ 46. Professional Habits (Workplace)
☐ 47. Rapport With Students
☐ 48. Record Keeping
☐ 49. Reflection
☐ 50. Relationships With Colleagues
☐ 51. Relationships With Parents and Community
☐ 52. School Climate
☐ 53. Self-Esteem (Students)
☐ 54. Self-Motivation (Students)
☐ 55. Special Needs (Special Education)
☐ 56. Standards and Practices
☐ 57. Student Behaviors
☐ 58. Students First
☐ 59. Supplemental Practices
☐ 60. Supporting Students
☐ 61. Teacher as Mentor
☐ 62. Technology (Professional Use)
☐ 63. Technology (Student Centered)
☐ 64. Test-Taking Skills
☐ 65. Time Management

TEACHER STRENGTHS	AREAS NEEDING IMPROVEMENT
1. _____	1. _____
2. _____	2. _____
3. _____	3. _____
4. _____	4. _____
5. _____	5. _____

EVALUATEE'S SIGNATURE: _____

EVALUATOR'S SIGNATURE: _____   DATE: _____/_____/_____

PERFORMANCE PROGRESS AND IMPROVEMENT PLAN

Teacher: _____   School: _____   **Page 3**

Grade/Department: _____

PART THREE: RECOMMENDATIONS FOR IMPROVEMENT/ACTION PLAN

TIME PERIOD: FROM _____ TO _____

CODE(S)   EVALUATOR'S SUGGESTIONS FOR IMPROVEMENT

TEACHER COMMENTS: (OPTIONAL)

Duplicate Page As Required

EVALUATEE'S SIGNATURE: _____

EVALUATOR'S SIGNATURE: _____   DATE: ____ /____ /_____

PERFORMANCE PROGRESS AND IMPROVEMENT PLAN

Teacher: _____   **School:** _____   **Page 4**

Grade/Department: _____

PART FOUR: SUMMATIVE REPORT

CODE(S)   TEACHER STRENGTH STATEMENT(S)

CODE(S)   SUGGESTIONS FOR IMPROVEMENT/ACTION PLANS

		S	NI	U

KEY: S = SATISFACTORY NI = NEEDS IMPROVEMENT U = UNSATISFACTORY

EVALUATEE'S SIGNATURE: _____

EVALUATOR'S SIGNATURE: _____   **DATE:** ____/____/_____

PERFORMANCE PROGRESS AND IMPROVEMENT PLAN

Teacher: _____   **School:** _____   **Page 5**

Grade/Department: _____

PART FIVE: PROFESSIONAL DEVELOPMENT REPORT

EVIDENCE*	WHERE ACQUIRED	EARNED HOURS	DATES

*ATTACH COPY OF TRANSCRIPT(S)/CERTIFICATE(S)

EVALUATOR'S COMMENTS: (OPTIONAL)

TEACHER'S COMMENTS: (OPTIONAL)

EVALUATEE'S SIGNATURE: _____

EVALUATOR'S SIGNATURE: _____   **DATE:** ____/____/_____

PART III

The Performance Progress and Improvement Plan

This section takes you through the entire process of completing the Performance Progress and Improvement Plan.

SECTION 4

Completing the Analysis of Teacher Performance

The administrator begins the teacher annual improvement report process by using the "65 Proficiency Categories" list (Section 1) and their proficiency assessment statements (Section 3) to record teacher strengths, areas needing improvement, and suggestions for improvement/action plans.

The steps to complete the "Analysis of Teacher Performance Form" follow:

Step 1: Complete the teacher identification information at the top of the form.

Step 2: From the 65 proficiency categories found at the top of the form, place a checkmark next to each category that reflects the teacher's strengths. Focus on those areas in which the teacher has shown sustained exemplary performance. Place the selected numbers on the "Strengths" row of the form.

Step 3: Repeat Steps 2 and 3 for "Areas Needing Improvement." (Different color pens may be used to differentiate between strengths and areas needing improvement).

Step 4*: Repeat Steps 2 and 3 for the "Suggestions for Improvement" row. You may then refer to the statements listed in the "650 Proficiency Assessment Statements" (Section 3) and record the letter of the statement that best reflects suggested action.

Note: You are not restricted to the categories listed in "Areas Needing Improvement" but can list appropriate statements found in other

---

* *Note:* Numbers indicate **categories**. Letters indicate **statements**.

categories as well. In addition, the vocabulary list found after each proficiency category may be used to edit the statements at will. The entire process can be completed in record time using the upgraded CD-ROM for this form and all the other forms in the "Performance Progress and Improvement Plan Packet."

In the following example, the ease with which the "Analysis of Teacher Performance Form" can be completed is apparent.

Figure 4.1   Sample "Analysis of Teacher Performance Form"

Strengths	37a	51j			
Areas Needing Improvement	57	30			
Suggestions for Improvement	60g	5c, h	11d	30e	

SECTION 5

Completing the Teacher Self-Assessment Form

The teacher has the opportunity to record self-reflections on teaching performance by completing the "Teacher Self-Assessment Form."

The teacher may either write in reflections on strengths and/or areas requiring improvement at the bottom of the form or use the 65 proficiency categories to specify (behaviors) in those areas.

Use of the glossary of terms (Section 2) helps the teacher categorize her reflections if she chooses to use the proficiency categories at the top of the form.

The steps to complete the "Teacher Self-Assessment Form" follow:

Step 1: Complete the teacher identification information at the top of the form.

Step 2: Fill in areas of strengths and areas needing improvement using one's own words. Alternatively, by using the 65 proficiency categories listed at the top of the form (along with the glossary of terms), place a checkmark next to each category that reflects a strength and a checkmark next to each category that reflects an area needing improvement. At this point, transfer the titles of the chosen categories to the "Strengths" and "Areas Needing Improvement" boxes. (Different color pens may be used to differentiate between strengths and areas needing improvement.)

In the example shown in Figure 5.1, the two approaches to completing the "Teacher Self-Assessment Form" are shown.

On the upper lines of the form, the teacher records strengths and areas needing improvement by writing them in the respective areas.

On the lower lines, the teacher uses the proficiency categories model to record Personal Attributes (37) as a strength and Behavior Modification (5) as an area needing improvement.

Figure 5.1   Sample "Teacher Self-Assessment Form"

Strengths	Areas Needing Improvement
1. *Perfect attendance record*	1. *Class control* _____
2. _____	2. _____
or	or
1. _____ *37* _____	1. _____ *5* __
2. _____	2. _____

This form is completed and submitted to the administrator prior to the first meeting regarding the annual performance report.

This form comprises the teacher's input at the beginning of the process of formulating the improvement plan.

SECTION 6

Completing the Recommendations for Improvement/Action Plan

In Part Three*, the administrator brings over the codes from Part One ("Areas Needing Improvement") and records the numbers corresponding to categories and letters corresponding to statements into the Code box. The text of the statement can then be written in the "Evaluator's Suggestions for Improvement" area.

Figure 6.1 Sample "Evaluator's Suggestions for Improvement"

Code	Evaluator's Suggestions for Improvement
60g	Encourage students to strive for greater achievement.
5c	Hold students accountable for their actions.
5h	Develop and implement classroom activities that engage students and deflect the possibility of their participating in acting-out behaviors.
11d	Attend workshops that provide creative approaches to lesson activities.
30e	Show students the link between school achievement and attaining lifetime goals.

---

* *Note:* It must be noted that each time the administrator/teacher team meets to track progress, a Part Three form may be generated. Plans may need to be redefined, modified, eliminated, or added to. The "Time Period" area at the top of the form provides the timetable for each review period. Nontenured teachers and/or those requiring extra support may require frequent review and adjustment and/or refinements of strategies, while others may require fewer review sessions. Thus, the final packet may include several Page 3 segments that become a part of the overall improvement package.

SECTION 7

Completing the Summative Report

Part Four, the "Summative Report," is completed at the culmination of the reporting process.

The administrator brings over the codes from Part One, "Strengths," and records the numbers corresponding to categories and letters corresponding to statements into the Code box (an optional step). The text of the statement can then be written in the "Strengths" area.

Note: Transferring the actual codes is optional, but this step is taken to provide the evaluator with a ready reference and to facilitate the smooth transition of the statements as selected.

Figure 7.1 Sample "Strength Statement(s)"

Code	Strength Statement(s)
37a	Extend the school workday beyond limits of closing schedule.
51j	Networks with students and families through community involvement.

The same process is followed for Part Two, "Suggestions for Improvement/ Action Plans."

After the codes and statements are inserted, the administrator rates the level of success the teacher reached in carrying out the action plans.

Figure 7.2 Sample "Suggestions for Improvement/Action Plans"

Code	Suggestions for Improvement/Action Plans	S	NI	U
60g	Encourage students to strive for greater achievement.	X		
5c	Hold students accountable for their actions.	X		
5h	Develop and implement classroom activities that engage students and deflect the possibility of their participating in acting-out behaviors.	X		
11d	Attend workshops that provide creative approaches to lesson activities.	X		
30e	Show students the link between school achievement and attaining lifetime goals.	X		

Assignment of ratings is based on a number of variables observed during the school year, including, but not limited to, student standardized test data/grades/portfolios, lesson plans reflecting well-thought-out and engaging activities, teacher informal assessments and formal evaluations, student behavior, attendance, and quality of completed assignments, proof of successful completion of professional improvement initiatives, parental communication, etc.

Any plan receiving an NI or U rating is carried over into the next annual performance plan along with the implementation of any other steps the district and administrator require.

SECTION 8

Completing the Professional Development Report

In this section, the teacher provides a record of professional development activities engaged in during the school year.

The teacher lists specific courses, workshops, etc. attended; where and when they were attended; credits earned; and so forth in the appropriate areas on the report.

To finalize the plan, both administrator and teacher are given the opportunity to enter a final comment on any aspect of the report.

Upon the completion of Part Five, the "Performance Progress and Improvement Plan" gives both the administrator and the teacher a comprehensive, ongoing record of achievement/growth for the school year and a platform onto which the plans for the coming year can be built.

Figure 8.1   Sample "Performance Progress and Improvement Plan"

Evidence	Where Acquired	Earned Hours	Dates
Certificate of Attendance—Elms Creative Literacy Conference	Fleetwood Institute	——	00/00/00
Mini-Course: The Creative Instructor	Genevieve College	1	Fall Semester

Figure 8.2   Evaluator's Comments* (Optional)

[Teacher's name] is to be commended for attaining a 100 percent attendance record during the 0000 school year.
Her attendance set an example for her students to emulate.

Figure 8.3   Teacher's Comments (Optional)

N.A.

* *Note:* The administrator incorporates the teacher's response of "Perfect Attendance Record" from the "Strengths" section of the "Teacher Self-Assessment Form" (see Figure 5.1).

PART IV

The Document in Action

This section contains examples of

- writing suggestions for improvement/action plans; and
- a sample Performance Progress and Improvement Plan.

SECTION 9

Writing Suggestions for Improvement/Action Plans

Other than being acknowledged and valued for the good that they bring to their students as a result of their dedication and performance, teachers are most interested in how they can demonstrate even greater proficiency in their craft.

To remain current and be able to meet the escalating challenges that the 21st century presents, education professionals must continuously evolve upwardly . . . in both knowledge and in skill.

Teachers must assume responsibility for critiquing their performance and for truly being lifelong learners.

It is the duty of administrators and supervisors to observe, quantify, and support the teacher's professional performance and growth, accessing a range of variables to do so.

Writing Year-End Teacher Improvement Plans—Right Now!! offers a method by which the process of chronicling yearly performance and planning for the coming year is accomplished quickly, efficiently, professionally, and easily.

This guide does not promote a set program that may or may not be a successful model of action for the user's district. The benefit of using this guide is its adaptability for use with any district performance assessment tool.

It is left to the expertise and on-site observations and evaluations of the user to customize the performance report, using the guide to support and facilitate those efforts.

To illustrate its use, several examples of improvement/action plans follow.

EXAMPLE #1: SECOND-GRADE NONTENURED TEACHER

Areas Needing Improvement

1. Curriculum Knowledge (Category 14)

Suggestions for Improvement/Action Plan

1. Enhance student learning through shared planning with colleagues regarding the Piedmont Stepping Up Reading Program. (9g)

2. Review and absorb the entire year's curriculum goals at the beginning of the term. (14c)

3. Utilize grade-level core curriculum guides as the basis for planning. (14d)

4. Remain open to replicating proven methods of planning to enhance teaching performance. (34b)

Note: In this example, half the statements are taken directly from the guide without editing. Statement #1 includes a specific program. Statement #4 specifies methods "of planning."

EXAMPLE #2: SEVENTH-GRADE SCIENCE TEACHER

Areas Needing Improvement

1. Critical Thinking: Expose students to thinking and reasoning by infusing these skills into lessons. (Category 12, Statement f)

Suggestions for Improvement/Action Plan

1. Organize lessons so that critical thinking is a natural extension of lesson activities, optimally during the last third of the scheduled period. (12i)

2. Require students to share their reasoning processes by elaborating on their answers and by working through the "Cause and Effect" section following each textbook unit. (12g)

3. Increase student performance in problem solving through their work in cooperative learning groups. (10h)

Note: In this example, adding clinical observations makes the prescribed actions more specific.

EXAMPLE #3: INSTRUMENTAL MUSIC TEACHER

Areas Needing Improvement

1. Time Management (Category 65)

2. Organization (Category 35)

Suggestions for Improvement/Action Plan

1. Maximize instructional time by effectively preparing materials and delegating tasks. (65b)

2. Utilize the Dopler Universal Computer Software program to organize instrument inventory, sheet music, and a schedule of individualized instruction. (35j)

3. Extend the school preparation day beyond the limits of the opening/closing schedule to facilitate your request to organize a school band. (37a)

4. Require students to share responsibility for maintaining the common areas in the music room, including the new concert addition. (39g)

Note: Customizing the statements is an important step in effectively completing year-end improvement plans when using the guide. The action plans in the example are taken from a variety of categories in the guide, and specifics based on clinical observation, materials, and the particular school site are incorporated.

The more you use *Writing Year-End Teacher Improvement Plans—Right Now!!,* the more uses you will find for it.

Complete annual performance reports in a fraction of the time they used to take but with 100 percent of the quality that you require.

SECTION 10

Sample Performance Progress and Improvement Plan

Teacher Profile:

For the past 3 of the 15 years Ms. Dell has been teaching at the Recognition Elementary School, she has served as the advisor to the school's junior cheerleading team. She enjoys them, and they adore her.

For the last 6 years of her 15-year tenure, Ms. Dell has taught third grade. Seventy to 75 percent of her students score at or above grade level on the state standardized tests in reading, with a slightly lower success rate in mathematics.

Near the end of the previous school year, the principal announced that the district had adopted a new math series and its concept(s) would be entirely different from those of other mathematics programs previously introduced.

Rote learning, practice sheets, and long columns of repetitive number facts were now things of the past.

Many of the teachers, including Ms. Dell, felt that this change would not only interfere with their record of success and nullify their familiarity with the content of the regular math program they had come to love, but truthfully, it would also take them out of their comfort zone.

After a year of using the program, Ms. Dell likes it even less and feels that the time spent setting up centers filled with manipulatives takes needed time away from more valuable work.

She also worries that her students' math scores on standardized tests will suffer.

PERFORMANCE PROGRESS AND IMPROVEMENT PLAN

Teacher: _Ms. Cora Dell_   **School:** _Recognition Elementary School_   **Page 1**

Grade/Department: _3_

PART ONE: ANALYSIS OF TEACHER PERFORMANCE
65 PROFICIENCY CATEGORIES

- ☐ 1. Accountability
- ☐ 2. Administration
- ☐ 3. Affective Domain
- ☐ 4. Assessment
- ☐ 5. Behavior Modification
- ☐ 6. Brain-Based Learning
- ☐ 7. Clarity
- ☐ 8. Closure
- ☐ 9. Collaboration
- ☐ 10. Cooperative Learning
- ☐ 11. Creativity
- ☐ 12. Critical Thinking
- ☐ 13. Curriculum Delivery
- ☐ 14. Curriculum Knowledge (Knowledge of Content)
- ☐ 15. Curriculum Management
- ☐ 16. Discipline (Classroom Management)
- ☐ 17. Evaluation
- ☐ 18. Extracurricular Activities
- ☐ 19. Feedback to Students
- ☐ 20. Goal Setting for Students
- ☐ 21. Guidance
- ☐ 22. Instructional Delivery
- ☐ 23. Instructional Diversity
- ☐ 24. Leadership Skills
- ☐ 25. Learning Styles (Multiple Intelligences)
- ☐ 26. Lesson Objectives
- ☐ 27. Managing Academic Diversity
- ☐ 28. Mandated Programs
- ☐ 29. Materials
- ☐ 30. Motivating Students
- ☐ 31. Motivating Students (Professional Practices)
- ☐ 32. Multiculturalism
- ☐ 33. Noninstructional Duties
- ☐ 34. Nontenured Teacher
- ☐ 35. Organization
- ☐ 36. Parents as Partners
- ☐ 37. Personal Attributes
- ☐ 38. Physical Plant (Creativity/Aesthetics)
- ☐ 39. Physical Plant (Instructional Space)
- ☐ 40. Planning (Lesson Plans)
- ☐ 41. Preparation for Delivery of Instruction
- ☐ 42. Preparation for Learning
- ☐ 43. Problem-Based Learning
- ☐ 44. Professional Development
- ☐ 45. Professional Habits (Personal)
- ☐ 46. Professional Habits (Workplace)
- ☐ 47. Rapport With Students
- ☐ 48. Record Keeping
- ☐ 49. Reflection
- ☐ 50. Relationships With Colleagues
- ☐ 51. Relationships With Parents and Community
- ☐ 52. School Culture
- ☐ 53. Self-Esteem (Students)
- ☐ 54. Self-Motivation (Students)
- ☐ 55. Special Needs (Special Education)
- ☐ 56. Standards and Practices
- ☐ 57. Student Behaviors
- ☐ 58. Students First
- ☐ 59. Supplemental Practices
- ☐ 60. Supporting Students
- ☐ 61. Teacher as Mentor
- ☐ 62. Technology (Professional Use)
- ☐ 63. Technology (Student Centered)
- ☐ 64. Test-Taking Skills
- ☐ 65. Time Management

TEACHER STRENGTHS	47	21			
AREAS NEEDING IMPROVEMENT	28				
SUGGESTIONS FOR IMPROVEMENT	15f	28g	42c	46b	65i

EVALUATEE'S SIGNATURE: _____

EVALUATOR'S SIGNATURE: _____ **DATE:** ___/___/___

PERFORMANCE PROGRESS AND IMPROVEMENT PLAN

Teacher: _Ms. Cora Dell_　　　　**School:** _Recognition Elementary School_　　**Page 2**

Grade/Department: _____3_____

PART TWO: TEACHER SELF-ASSESSMENT FORM

65 PROFICIENCY CATEGORIES

☐ 1. Accountability
☐ 2. Administration
☐ 3. Affective Domain
☐ 4. Assessment
☐ 5. Behavior Modification
☐ 6. Brain-Based Learning
☐ 7. Clarity
☐ 8. Closure
☐ 9. Collaboration
☐ 10. Cooperative Learning
☐ 11. Creativity
☐ 12. Critical Thinking
☐ 13. Curriculum Delivery
☐ 14. Curriculum Knowledge (Knowledge of Content)
☐ 15. Curriculum Management
☐ 16. Discipline (Classroom Management)
☐ 17. Evaluation
☐ 18. Extracurricular Activities
☐ 19. Feedback to Students
☐ 20. Goal Setting for Students
☐ 21. Guidance
☐ 22. Instructional Delivery
☐ 23. Instructional Diversity

☐ 24. Leadership Skills
☐ 25. Learning Styles (Multiple Intelligences)
☐ 26. Lesson Objectives
☐ 27. Managing Academic Diversity
☐ 28. Mandated Programs
☐ 29. Materials
☐ 30. Motivating Students
☐ 31. Motivating Students (Professional Practices)
☐ 32. Multiculturalism
☐ 33. Noninstructional Duties
☐ 34. Nontenured Teacher
☐ 35. Organization
☐ 36. Parents as Partners
☐ 37. Personal Attributes
☐ 38. Physical Plant (Creativity/Aesthetics)
☐ 39. Physical Plant (Instructional Space)
☐ 40. Planning (Lesson Plans)
☐ 41. Preparation for Delivery of Instruction
☐ 42. Preparation for Learning
☐ 43. Problem-Based Learning

☐ 44. Professional Development
☐ 45. Professional Habits (Personal)
☐ 46. Professional Habits (Workplace)
☐ 47. Rapport With Students
☐ 48. Record Keeping
☐ 49. Reflection
☐ 50. Relationships With Colleagues
☐ 51. Relationships With Parents and Community
☐ 52. School Climate
☐ 53. Self-Esteem (Students)
☐ 54. Self-Motivation (Students)
☐ 55. Special Needs (Special Education)
☐ 56. Standards and Practices
☐ 57. Student Behaviors
☐ 58. Students First
☐ 59. Supplemental Practices
☐ 60. Supporting Students
☐ 61. Teacher as Mentor
☐ 62. Technology (Professional Use)
☐ 63. Technology (Student Centered)
☐ 64. Test-Taking Skills
☐ 65. Time Management

TEACHER STRENGTHS	AREAS NEEDING IMPROVEMENT
1. Jr. Cheerleaders advisor	1. _____65_____
2. Use of computer	2.
3.	3.
4.	4.
5.	5.

EVALUATEE'S SIGNATURE: _____

EVALUATOR'S SIGNATURE: _____　**DATE:** ____/____/_____

PERFORMANCE PROGRESS AND IMPROVEMENT PLAN

Teacher: _Ms. Cora Dell_   **School:** _Recognition Elementary School_   **Page 3**

Grade/Department: _____3_____

PART THREE: RECOMMENDATIONS FOR IMPROVEMENT/ACTION PLAN

TIME PERIOD: FROM ___00/00___ TO ___00/00___

CODE(S)   EVALUATOR'S SUGGESTIONS FOR IMPROVEMENT

15f	Follow approved district program guides when planning instruction.
28g	Participate fully in school/districtwide professional development activities.
42c	Start each math lesson by conducting a review of prior learning related to a real-life topic, as suggested in the new Math Two-Four program guidebook.
46b	Remain flexible and receptive to the use of new materials and programs.
65i	Utilize preparation periods for planning and implementing real-life scenarios and use of manipulatives in the math program.

TEACHER COMMENTS: (OPTIONAL)

Duplicate Page As Required

EVALUATEE'S SIGNATURE: _____

EVALUATOR'S SIGNATURE: _____   **DATE:** ____/____/_____

PERFORMANCE PROGRESS AND IMPROVEMENT PLAN

Teacher: _Ms. Cora Dell_   **School:** _Recognition Elementary School_   **Page 4**

Grade/Department: _3_

PART FOUR: SUMMATIVE REPORT

CODE(S)   TEACHER STRENGTH STATEMENT(S)

47c	Ms. Dell connects with her students by showing a personal interest in their concerns.
21c	Served as Jr. Cheerleader advisor, 0000 to the present, for junior cheerleading students. Ms. Dell volunteered to give parent workshops on how to use the computer to help their children complete and review homework assignments.

CODE(S)   SUGGESTIONS FOR IMPROVEMENT/ACTION PLANS

		S	NI	U
15f	Follow approved district program guides when planning instruction.	X		
28g	Participate fully in school/districtwide professional development activities.	X		
42c	Start each math lesson by conducting a review of prior learning related to a real-life topic, as suggested in the new Math Two-Four program guidebook.	X		
46b	Remain flexible and receptive to the use of new materials and programs.		X	
65i	Utilize preparation periods for planning and implementing real-life scenarios and use of manipulatives in the math program.		X	

KEY: S = SATISFACTORY NI = NEEDS IMPROVEMENT U = UNSATISFACTORY

EVALUATEE'S SIGNATURE: _____

EVALUATOR'S SIGNATURE: _____ DATE: ____/____/_____

PERFORMANCE PROGRESS AND IMPROVEMENT PLAN

Teacher: Ms. Cora Dell   **School:** Recognition Elementary School   **Page 5**

Grade/Department: _____3_____

PART FIVE: PROFESSIONAL DEVELOPMENT REPORT

EVIDENCE*	WHERE ACQUIRED	EARNED HOURS	DATES
Attended district math workshop. (certificate attached)	Frontbridge Middle School	---	00/00

*ATTACH COPY OF TRANSCRIPT(S)/CERTIFICATE(S)

EVALUATOR'S COMMENTS: (OPTIONAL)

TEACHER'S COMMENTS: (OPTIONAL)

I plan to work with my fellow third-grade teachers on planning and setting up activity tables for the math program.

EVALUATEE'S SIGNATURE: _____

EVALUATOR'S SIGNATURE: _____ **DATE:** ____/____/_____